brain droppings

brain droppings

GEORGE CARLIN

HYPERION

NEW YORK

A leather-bound, signed first edition of this book has been published by
The Easton Press.

Copyright © 1997, Comedy Concepts, Inc.

Book Design by Spinning Egg Design Group, Inc.

Library of Congress Cataloging-in-Publication Data

Carlin, George.
Brain droppings / George Carlin.
p.   cm.
ISBN 0-7868-6313-7
1. American wit and humor. I. Title.
PN6162.C275 1997
818´.5402—dc21   96-52373
CIP

Paperback ISBN: 0-7868-8321-9

FIRST PAPERBACK EDITION
24 25 26 27 28 29 30

This book is dedicated to my big brother Patrick,
who was kind enough to teach me attitude.

ACKNOWLEDGMENTS

I would like to acknowledge the invaluable assistance and direction I received from my (very first) editor in assembling this book. Laurie Abkemeier took the many disparate items I turned in and somehow fashioned a coherent book. Her calm, professional style also helped keep my inner maniac somewhat in check. Somewhat. Thank you, Laurie.

This would also be a good time to acknowledge and express gratitude for the wise and careful guidance my career has received over the past 15 years from Jerry Hamza. His judgment, generosity, and belief in my career's long-term potential have helped me reach a level I never expected. It isn't often a performer can say his manager is also his best friend. I can. By the way, it helps a little that Jerry's inner maniac is even weirder than mine.

And finally, a sincere thank you to my first boss in radio, Joe Monroe, who, when I was 18, told me always to write down my ideas and save them. He also gave me my start. Thanks, buddy.

"There is a vitality, a life force, a quickening that is translated through you into action, and because there is only one of you in all time, this expression is unique. And if you block it, it will never exist through any other medium and be lost. The world will not have it. It is not your business to determine how good it is, nor how valuable it is, nor how it compares with other expressions. It is your business to keep it yours clearly and directly, to keep the channel open. You do not even have to believe in yourself or your work. You have to keep yourself open and aware directly to the urges that motivate you. Keep the channel open. . . .

"No artist is pleased. . . . [There is no] satisfaction whatever at any time. There is only a queer, divine dissatisfaction, a blessed unrest that keeps us marching and makes us more alive than the others."

—Martha Graham to Agnes de Mille, *Martha: The Life and Work of Martha Graham*

"We shall never understand one another until we reduce the language to seven words."

—Kahlil Gibran, *Sand and Foam*

PREFACE

For a long time, my stand-up material has drawn from three sources. The first is the English language: words, phrases, sayings, and the ways we speak. The second source, as with most comedians, has been what I think of as the "little world," those things we all experience every day: driving, food, pets, relationships, and idle thoughts. The third area is what I call the "big world": war, politics, race, death, and social issues. Without having actually measured, I would say this book reflects that balance very closely.

The first two areas will speak for themselves, but concerning the "big world," let me say a few things.

I'm happy to tell you there is very little in this world that I believe in. Listening to the comedians who comment on political, social, and cultural issues, I notice most of their material reflects an underlying belief that somehow things were better once and that with just a little effort we could set them right again. They're looking for solutions, and rooting for particular results, and I think that necessarily limits the tone and substance of what they say. They're talented and funny people, but they're nothing more than cheerleaders attached to a specific, wished-for outcome.

I don't feel so confined. I frankly don't give a fuck how it all turns out in this country—or anywhere else, for that matter. I think the human game was up a long time ago (when the high priests and traders took over), and now we're just playing out the string. And that is, of course, precisely what I find so amusing: the slow circling of the drain by a once promising species, and the sappy, ever-more-desperate belief in this country that there is actually some sort of "American Dream," which has merely been misplaced.

The decay and disintegration of this culture is astonishingly amusing if you are emotionally detached from it. I have always viewed it from a safe distance, knowing I don't belong; it doesn't include me, and it never has. No matter how you care to define it, **I do not identify with the local group.** Planet, species, race, nation, state, religion, party, union, club, association, neighborhood improvement committee; I have no interest in any of it. I love and treasure individuals as I meet them, I loathe and despise the groups they identify with and belong to.

So, if you read something in this book that sounds like advocacy of a particular political point of view, please reject the notion. My interest in "issues" is merely to point out how badly we're doing, not to suggest a way we might do better. Don't confuse me with those who cling to hope. I enjoy describing how things are, I have no interest in how they "ought to be." And I certainly have no interest in fixing them. I sincerely believe that if you think there's a solution, you're part of the problem. My motto: Fuck Hope!

P.S.   Lest you wonder, personally, I am a joyful individual with a long, happy marriage and a close and loving family. My career has turned out better than I ever dreamed, and it continues to expand. I am a personal optimist but a skeptic about all else. What may sound to some like anger is really nothing more than sympathetic contempt. I view my species with a combination of wonder and pity, and I root for its destruction. And please don't confuse my point of view with cynicism; the real cynics are the ones who tell you everything's gonna be all right.

P.P.S.   By the way, if, by some chance, you folks do manage to straighten things out and make everything better, I still don't wish to be included.

brain droppings

PEOPLE AHEAD OF ME ON LINE

Here's something I can do without: People ahead of me on the supermarket line who are paying for an inexpensive item by credit card or personal check. People! Take my word for this: Tic Tacs is not a major purchase. And, I get just as discouraged when a guy who's buying a simple jar of spaghetti sauce tries to pay with a letter of credit from the Bank of Liechtenstein. Folks, carry some fuckin' money around, will ya? It comes in handy! No one should be borrowing money from a bank at 18 percent interest to buy a loaf of bread.

And what about these cretins at the airport gift shop who think somehow they're in the Mall of America? It's an airport! I'm standin' there with one newspaper and a pack of gum; I gotta get to my plane. Why does the genetic defective ahead of me choose this moment to purchase a complete set of dishes and a new fall wardrobe? What is this, fuckin' Macy's? And of course, the clerk lady has to carefully wrap each dish separately, but she's working real fast—because she's eighty-nine!! Plus she's from Sri Lanka. The rural part. And now dishman wants to know if it's okay to use Turkish traveler's checks. You know what I do? I steal things. Fuck 'em! I grab a handful of candy bars and six magazines and head for the gate. My attitude? It wasn't their stuff to begin with.

PEOPLE WHO SHOULD BE PHASED OUT

{ } Guys who always harmonize the last few notes of "Happy Birthday."

{ } People over 40 who can't put on reading glasses without making self-conscious remarks about their advancing age.

{ } Guys who wink when they're kidding.

{ } Men who propose marriage on the giant TV screen at a sports stadium.

{ } Guys in their fifties who flash me the peace sign and really mean it.

{ } People with a small patch of natural white hair who think it makes them look interesting.

{ } Guys with creases in their jeans.

{ } People who know a lot of prayers by heart.

{ } People who move their lips—when *I'm* talking!

{ } Guys who want to shake my hand even though we just saw each other an hour ago.

{ } A celebrity couple who adopt a Third-World baby and call it Rain Forest.

{ } Guys who wear suits all day and think an earring makes them cool at night.

{ } Old people who tell me what the weather used to be where they used to live.

❨❩ Men who have one long, uninterrupted eyebrow.

❨❩ Guys who wink and give me the peace sign simultaneously.

❨❩ People who say, "Knock knock," when entering a room and, "Beep beep," when someone is in their path.

❨❩ Fat guys who laugh at everything.

❨❩ People who have memorized a lot of TV-show theme songs and are really proud of it.

❨❩ Women who think it's cute to have first names consisting solely of initials.

❨❩ People who give their house or car a name.

❨❩ People who give their genitals a name.

❨❩ Guys who can juggle, but only a little bit.

✖ Actors who drive race cars.

❨❩ Men who wear loafers without socks. Especially if they have creases in their jeans.

❨❩ Athletes and coaches who give more than a hundred percent.

❨❩ Guys who still smell like their soap in the late afternoon.

❨❩ Blind people who don't want any help.

✖ Guys who wear their watches on the inside of their wrists.

❨❩ Any man who wears a suit and tie to a ballgame.

❨❩ Guys who flash me the thumbs-up sign. Especially if they're winking and making the peace sign with the other hand.

SEVEN THINGS I'M TIRED OF

I'm gettin' tired of guys who smoke pipes. When are they gonna outlaw this shit? Guy with a fuckin' pipe! It's an arrogant thing to place a burning barrier between you and the rest of the world. It's supposed to imply thoughtfulness or intelligence. It's not intelligent to stand around with a controlled fire sticking out of your mouth. I say, "Hey, professor! You want somethin' hot to suck on? Call me! I'll give ya somethin' to put in your mouth!" I think these pipe-smokers oughta just move to the next level and go ahead and suck a dick. There's nothing wrong with suckin' dicks. Men do it, women do it; can't be all bad if everybody's doin' it. I say, Drop the pipe, and go to the dick! That's my advice. I'm here to help.

I'm also sick of car alarms. Not the screeching and beeping; that doesn't bother me. It's just the idea of a car alarm that I find offensive. Especially the ones that talk to you: "Move away! Move away!" "Ohhhh? Really!" That's when I reach for my sharpest key. And I put a deep gouge in that paint job, all the way 'round the car. Three hundred and sixty degrees. I might even make two trips around, if I don't have a luncheon appointment that day. And then I walk away slowly, unconcerned about the screeching and beeping, because I know that no one takes car alarms seriously. Car alarms are a Yuppie-boomer conceit, and they're responsible for most of the carjacking that's going on. Car alarms and The Club have have made it harder for thieves to steal parked cars, and so instead they're stealing cars with people in them, and people are dying. And it's all because these selfish, boomer degenerates can't stand to part with their personal property. Fuck boomers, and fuck their pussified car alarms!

I'm also sick of having to look at bearded guys who don't know how to trim the lower edges of their beards, where they extend back toward the neck. They trim too far up toward the chin, leaving a glaring, fleshy strip where there ought to be hair. Guys, you need to let the beard extend far enough back under your chin, so it reaches the point where your neck begins. Then, from the fold or angle that forms between your jaw and neck, you shave down-ward. If you don't have that fold; if you have a fat, fleshy pouch under your jaw with no definition, you shouldn't be trimming your beard at all. You should let it grow long and bushy, so it covers that goofy-looking pouch.

And I've just about had it with all these geeky fucks who walk around listening to Walkmans. What are these jack-offs telling us? They're too good to participate in daily life? They're sealing themselves off? Big fuckin' loss. And what is it they're listening to that's so compelling? I think a person has to be fairly uncomfortable with his thoughts to have the need to block them out while simply walking around. I'd love to know how many of these obviously disturbed people become suicides.

I've also grown weary of reading about clouds in a book. Doesn't this piss you off? You're reading a nice story, and suddenly the writer has to stop and describe the clouds. Who cares? I'll bet you anything I can write a decent novel, with a good, entertaining story, and never once mention the clouds. Really! Every book you read, if there's an outdoor scene, an open window, or even a door slightly ajar, the writer has to say, "As Bo and Velma walked along the shore, the clouds hung ponderously on the horizon like steel-gray, loosely formed gorilla turds." I'm not interested. Skip the clouds and get to the fucking. The only story I know of where clouds were important was Noah's Ark.

And I don't appreciate being put on hold and being forced to listen to someone else's radio. I don't even listen to my own radio, why should I have to pay money to call some company and listen to theirs? And it's always that same shit, soft rock! That sucky, non-threatening, easy-listening pussy music. Soft rock is an oxymoron. Furthermore, it's not rock, and it's not even music. It's just soft.

I'm tired of being unable to buy clothing that doesn't have writing and printing all over it. Insipid sayings, pseudo-wisdom, cute slogans, team logos, designer names, brand trademarks, small-business ego trips; the marketing pigs and advertising swine have turned us all into walking billboards. You see some asshole walkin' by, and he's got on a fruity Dodger hat and a Hard Rock Cafe T-shirt. Of course you can't see the shirt if he's wearing his hot-shit Chicago Bulls jacket. The one that only 50 million other loser jock-sniffers own. And since this cretinous sports fan/consumer zombie is completely for sale to anyone, he rounds out his ensemble with FedEx sneakers, ValuJet socks, *Wall Street Journal* sweatpants, a Starbucks jock strap, and a Microsoft condom with Bill Gates's head on the end of it. No one in this country owns his personal appearance anymore. America has become a nation of obedient consumers, actively participating in their own degradation.

A FEW THINGS I LIKE

✖ A guy who doesn't know what he's doing and won't admit it.

❴ ❵ A permanently disfigured gun collector.

❴ ❵ A whole lotta people tap dancing at once.

❴ ❵ When a big hole opens up in the ground.

❴ ❵ The third week in February.

❴ ❵ Guys who say "cock-a-roach."

❴ ❵ A woman with no feet, because she's not always nagging you to take her dancing.

KEEP IT CLEAN

I never wash my hands after using a public restroom. Unless something gets on me. Otherwise, I figure I'm as clean as when I walked in. Besides, the sink is usually filthier than I am. I'm convinced that many of the men I see frantically washing up do not do the same thing at home. Americans are obsessed with appearances and have an unhealthy fixation on cleanliness. Relax, boys. It's only your dick. If it's so dirty that after handling it you need to wash your hands, you may as well just go ahead and scrub your dick while you're at it. Tell the truth. Wouldn't you like to see some guy trying to dry his genitals with one of those forced-air blowing machines that are mounted four feet off the ground?

G.C.'S GUIDE TO DINING OUT

RESTAURANTS

There are certain clues that tell you how much a restaurant will cost. If the word *cuisine* appears in the advertising, it will be expensive. If they use the word *food*, it will be moderately priced. However, if the sign says *eats*, even though you'll save some money on food, your medical bills may be quite high.

I don't like trendy food. When I hear, "sauteed boneless panda groin," I know I'm in the wrong place. There's such a thing as pretentious food. Puree of woodchuck, marinated bat nipples, weasel chops, porcupine cacciatore. Or fried eagle. A guy said to me recently, "C'mon, we'll go to Baxter's, they have really great fried eagle." I'm thinkin' to myself, "Do I really wanna know this guy?"

However, if you *are* going to dine with pretentious people, here are some items you can order that are sure to impress: deep-dish moose balls, diced yak, badger gumbo, gorilla fondue, filet of hyena, jackal tartare, rack of prairie dog, free-range mole en brochette, wolf noodle soup, loin of chipmunk, curried woodpecker, stir-fried weasel, penguin scallopini, sweet-and-sour loon heads, whale chowder, toasted snail penises, koala flambé, wombat souvlaki, grenadine of mule, and candied goat anus.

Then, at the other end of the spectrum, there is the decidedly nontrendy restaurant, where the special sometimes is simply "meat." Big sign in the window: "Today's special: Meat."

"I'll have the meat."

"Would you like sauce with that?"

"What kind of sauce would that be?"

"That would be meat sauce."

It's similar to a fish sandwich. Have you ever seen these places that feature "fish sandwiches"? I always think, "Well, that's kind of general." I mean, I wouldn't order something called a "meat sandwich," would you?" At least not without a couple of follow-up questions: "Does anyone know where this meat came from?" "Are any of the waitresses missing?"

DEALING WITH THE WAITER

I think when you eat out you should have a little fun; it's good for digestion. Simple things. After the waiter recites a long list of specials, ask him if they serve cow feet.

But act really interested in the specials. When he says, "Today we have goat-cheese terrine with arugula juice, sautéed cod with capers and baby vegetables, coastal shrimp cooked in spiced carrot juice, roast free-range chicken with ginger and chickpea fries, and duck breast in truffle juice," act like you're completely involved. Say, "The cod. What is the cod sautéed in?" "A blend of canola and tomato oils." (No hurry here.) "Ahhh, yes! [pointing thoughtfully at the waiter] I'll have the grilled cheese sandwich."

Even some low-end places are pretentious. The menu can't merely say "cheeseburger." They have to get wordy. So, go along with them. When you order your food use their language. But you must look right at the waiter; no fair reading from the menu. Look him in the eye and say, "I'll have the succulent, fresh-ground, government-inspected, choice, all-beef, six-ounce patty on your own award-winning sesame-seed bun, topped with a generous slice of Wisconsin's finest Grade-A cheddar cheese made from only premium milk and poured from large, galvanized steel cans, having originally been extracted from a big, fat, smelly, champion blue-ribbon cow with a brain disease."

Continue that style with other items: Instead of asking for a glass of water, say you'd like a "cylindrical, machine-blown, clear drinking vessel filled with nature's own color-less, odorless, extra-wet, liquid water."

Have fun. Be difficult. Order unusual things: a chopped corn sandwich. Rye potato chips. Filet of bone with diced peas. Peanut butter and jellyfish. Ask for a glass of skim water. Insist on fried milk. Chocolate orange juice. Order a grilled gorgonzola cheese sandwich on whole-wheat ladyfingers. Then top the whole thing off with a bowl of food coloring and a large glass of saturated fat.

Issue special instructions. Ask for the French toast, medium rare. Get a pizza with no toppings, hold the crust. Tell 'em you want eggs: "Fry the whites and poach the yolks." Order a basket of poppy seed rolls and tell them to scrape off the seeds and put them in a separate bowl and heat them to 200 degrees. Keep them busy.

Tell your waiter you want to make a substitution: "Instead of my napkin, I'll have the lobster tails." See what he says. Ask him if the garnish is free. If it is, tell him all you're having is a large plate of garnish.

If they have a salad bar, ask how many times you can go back. If they say as many times as you like, ask for a lawn bag. Come back the next day with a small truck. Tell them you weren't quite finished eating the night before. You're actually within your legal rights, because, technically, no one is ever finished eating.

Ask him if the chef would mind preparing a dish that's not on the menu. Then describe something simple but unusual. Like half a coconut filled with egg whites. When the waiter comes back and says, "Yes, the chef said he will be delighted to make that for you," tell him, "Well, never mind, I don't like that anymore."

Giving the waiter your drink order can be fun. If you're alone, show the guy you're a real man. "Gimme a glass of napalm and paint thinner straight up." Be an individualist; order a gin and hot chocolate. If you're with a date, be sophisticated. Say, "I'll have a rum and goat juice with a twist of cucumber on dry ice." Always order your date's drink; that's very romantic. Especially if you're trying to get laid. "The lady will have a martini, a glass of wine, two zombies, and a beer. And do you have any quaaludes?"

By the way, if your date is complaining of constipation, order her a prune margarita with a twist of Feenamint.

When the food arrives, change your mind. Say, "I've changed my mind, waiter. Instead of the roast suckling pig, I believe I'll have a half order of Kellogg's Product 19."

And always, when the food arrives, send something back. It's considered very sophisticated. But make sure you use colorful language. Tell him, "Waiter, this veal tastes like the inside front panel of Ferdinand Magellan's shorts. And I'm referring to the first voyage."

Show him you're a man of new ideas. When he comes with the pepper mill, refuse the pepper, but tell him to sprinkle some dandruff on your food.

Actually, the pepper mill can be a source of great fun. Keep the waiter going on the pepper mill for a long time. Disturbingly long. Like, for about fifteen minutes. Until everyone in the restaurant is really uncomfortable. Then, when your food and silverware are completely covered with a thin layer of ground pepper, say, "Okay, stop! That's perfect!" Then, a few minutes later, call the waiter over and tell him, "This food has way too much pepper on it!"

Now that you have your food, the waiter can begin to ask you if everything is all right. "Is everything all right?" "Yes. Thank you. Good-bye!" Some waiters are very persistent. I had one call me at home the following day. "Did the food stay down?"

Usually, when they ask me if everything is all right, I'll tell them the truth. I say, "Well, I had a problem with the peas. I received 143 peas. Of them, 36 were overcooked, 27 were undercooked, and 18 were not quite the same color as the others."

Or I'll tell them more than they really want to know. "No, everything is not all right. I'm going through a period of upheaval. I have a rogue polyp in my bowel, my wife ran off with a periodontist, and my son has been arrested for defecating in a mall."

And always fill out the "How did we do?" card. It's very helpful to the owner. "Everything was wonderful, except the waiter had some vomit on his shoes and a tiny snot on the end of his nose. It was small, but it was definitely a snot."

I hope these pointers and suggestions will enhance your next experience dining out. Tell 'em George sent you.

FOOD TERMS

BREADSTICKS:

If drumsticks are for playing drums, you'd think breadsticks would be for playing bread, wouldn't you? "Would you like some breadsticks?" "No thank you. I don't play bread; I play drums. Perhaps I'll have a drum roll."

SHELLED PEANUTS:

Why don't shelled peanuts have shells? If you're clothed, you have clothes, so if you're shelled, you should have shells. You'd think they'd call peanuts without shells, "unshelled" peanuts, wouldn't you? Same goes for pitted prunes.

And boned chicken. I ask you, Where are the bones? I can't find them. In my opinion, it ought to be called *de*-boned chicken.

And what about semi-boneless ham? What's going on? Does it have only half a bone? Or does "semi-boneless ham" mean that some complete object that is not entirely a bone has been removed from the ham?

WAFFLE IRON:

Why on earth would you want to iron a waffle? Wouldn't that just flatten out all the little squares? No, I believe waffles should be dry cleaned. Pancakes, of course, should always be ironed.

OPENING YOUR OWN RESTAURANT

Everyone thinks they have a really good idea for a restaurant but I've heard some terrible schemes. I even had a few myself.

My first idea was: All You Can Eat for 60 Cents. That didn't work. So I went the other way: All You Can Eat for $1500. That didn't work either. Then I made my fatal mistake: All You Can Eat for Free. Closed after one meal.

My next idea was The Used Footwear Restaurant. Our slogan was, How Would You Like to Enjoy a Nice Hot Meal Eaten Out of Someone Else's Used Footwear? Somehow, it didn't work. Although, after I sold it, it became the very successful fast-food franchise, Beef in a Brogan.

Chili Alley was my favorite, and a lot of people got a kick out of it. It was a drive-through chili restaurant. And you didn't even have to slow down. You could drive through at speeds up to 40 miles an hour, and we would shoot the chili at you from a shotgun. Just two dollars. Both barrels, three-fifty. Dry cleaning extra.

Vinny's House of Toast. This was great. My partner Vinny and I tried to come up with 101 different ways to serve toast. Eventually, we could only settle on three. The first item was . . . toast. Basically, an order of toast. With something on it—butter, margarine, jelly, whatever. The second thing we came up with was . . . a double order of toast. That would be, of course, twice as much toast, along with double the butter, margarine, jelly, whatever. The only other thing we could think of was something I liked a lot: a toast sandwich. Usually on toast. We also tried Toast on a Bun, but the public wasn't ready. Too high-concept.

Then there was Bombs Away. This was an idea that should have worked. Patrons were seated on the ground floor; the kitchen was on the balcony. When your order was ready, you stood under the balcony holding a plate, and the chef dropped your food while everyone yelled, "Bombs away!" It worked great with steak and chops. But the idea began to unravel when we tried things like soup and creamed spinach. Peas were a definite problem, too.

My last unsuccessful attempt was The Top of the Schmuck. It was a ten-story statue of a schmuck wearing a cowboy hat, with a revolving restaurant in the hatband. The problem was, it rotated way too fast. People got sick just waiting for a table. But I still think the idea was basically sound.

Bon appétit.

GOBBLE THIS

On Thanksgiving at our house we like variety, so we don't have turkey every year. Last year we had a swan. It was nice; everyone got some neck. Another year we had a seagull. Delicious! It's a little fishy, but at least there's no need to add salt. Two years ago we had a stork. Lots of meat, but, Jesus, the wishbone makes a helluva noise. This year we're expecting a few people over, so we're having a flamingo. And I'm getting the leg that folds up. They say the meat is sweeter and more tender because the flamingo doesn't use it much.

WELL, YA GOTTA LIVE SOMEPLACE

I grew up in New York City and lived there until I was thirty.

At that time, I decided I'd had enough of life in a dynamic, sophisticated city, so I moved to Los Angeles. Actually, I moved there because of the time difference. I was behind in my work, and wanted to pick up the extra three hours. Technically, for the last thirty years I've been living in my own past.

I knew I didn't want to move to the Midwest. I could never live in a place where the outstanding geographic feature is the horizon. The Midwest seems like a nice place to catch up on your sleep.

Another reason I could never live in the Midwest is that it gets really cold there. You've heard of hypothermia and exposure? I could never be comfortable in a place where you can die simply by going out to the mailbox. Living in an area where an open window can cause death seems foolish to me.

Of course, living in the South was never an option—the main problem being they have too much respect for authority; they're soldier-sniffers and cop lovers. I don't respect that, and I could never live with it. There's also way too much religion in the South to be consistent with good mental health.

Still, I love traveling down there, especially when I'm in the mood for a quick trip to the thirteenth century. I'm not someone who buys all that "New South" shit you hear; I judge a place by the number of lynchings they've had, overall. Atlanta even found it necessary to come up with an apologetic civic slogan: Atlanta: The City Too Busy to Hate. I think they're trying to tell us something.

There's also the communications problem. I have trouble understanding Southerners. Some of them sound like they're chewing on a dick. And I really have nothing against them individually; one by one they can be quite charming. But when you take them as a whole, there's some really dangerous genetic material floating around down there.

So, I live in Los Angeles, and it's kind of a goofy place. They have an airport named after John Wayne. That ought to explain it. It has a charming kind of superstitious innocence.

But if you really want to understand life in California, forget the grief clinics and yogaholics. Forget biofeedback, Feldenkrais, neurolinguistic programming, and the Alexander technique.

Disregard spirit guides, centering groups, dream workshops, bioenergetics, pyramid energy, and primal therapy.

Ignore centering, fasting, Rolfing, grounding, channeling, rebirthing, nurturing, self-parenting, and colon cleansing.

And don't even think about polarity work, inversion swings, flower essences, guided synchronicity, harmonic brain wave synergy, and psychocalisthenics.

You also need pay no attention to nude volleyball, spinach therapy, white wine hot tubs, jogging on hot coals, and the people who sing Christmas carols to zoo animals.

Forget all that. The only thing you have to know about California is this: They have traffic school for chocaholics.

Okay?

California is the only place where you might hear someone

say, "Jason can't come to the phone, he's taking his wind lesson."

The problem most New Yorkers have with Los Angeles is that it is fragmented and lacks a vital center. The people have no common experience. Instead, they exude a kind of bemused detachment that renders them intensely uninteresting. The West Coast experience is soft and peripheral, New York is hard and concentrated. California is a small woman saying, "Fuck me." New York is a large man saying, "Fuck you!"

Still, I live in California. But I'm not "laid-back," and I'm certainly not "mellow." I associate those qualities with the comatose. The solar system wasn't formed because matter was laid-back; life didn't arise from the oceans and humans descend from the trees because DNA was mellow. It happened because of something called *energy.*

New York has energy, and all I can say is this: If you can't handle it, stay the fuck out. Living in New York is a character-builder; you must know who you are, what you're doing, where you're going, and how to get there. No bullshit tolerated! New York people are tough and resilient. All the rest of you are varying degrees of soft.

Most outsiders can't handle New York, so they wind up back in Big Loins, Arkansas, badmouthing The City for the rest of their lives. Actually, most of the people who run New York down have never been there. And if they ever went, we would destroy them in nine minutes. People hate New York, because that's where the action is, and they know it's passing them by. Most of the decisions that control people's lives are made in New York City. Not in Washington, not on Pennsylvania

Avenue. In New York City! Madison Avenue and Wall Street. People can't handle that. Pisses 'em off. Fuck 'em!

And I'm really glad the Yankees humiliated the Braves in the World Series. I'm glad the gritty, tough, Third-World, streetwise New York culture triumphed over the soft, suburban, wholesome, white-Christian, tacky mall culture of Atlanta. Overgrown small towns like Atlanta have no business in the major leagues in the first place.

Concerning L.A. versus New York: I have now lived half my life in each of America's two most hated, feared, and envied cities, and you want to know something? There's no comparison. New York even has a better class of assholes. Even the lames in New York have a certain appealing, dangerous quality.

As an example of how hopeless California is, when I first got there, a policeman gave me a ticket for jaywalking. You have to understand the kind of people who live in California. They are willing to stand, passive and inert, on a curb, when absolutely no traffic is coming, or maybe just a little traffic that could easily be dodged. They simply stand there obediently and wait for an electric light to give them permission to proceed. I couldn't believe this cop. I laughed at him. The ticket cost me about twenty dollars in 1966. Since that time, I figure I have jaywalked an additional thousand times or so without being caught. Fuck that lame-ass cop! I've managed to prorate that ticket down to about two cents a jaywalk.

One thing I find appealing in California is the emphasis on driving. I like to drive, I'm skillful at it, and I do it aggressively. And I don't mean I scream at people or flash them the finger. I simply go about my passage swiftly and silently, with a certain deliberate, dark efficiency. In the land of the unassertive, the aggressive man is king.

Of course, in Los Angeles, *everything* is based on driving, even the killings. In New York, most people don't have cars, so if you want to kill a person, you have to take the subway to their house. And sometimes on the way, the train is delayed and you get impatient, so you have to kill someone on the subway. That's why there are so many subway murders; no one has a car. Basically, if more people in New York had cars, the subways would be a lot safer.

I hope you can tell, the Apple is still number one in my heart. I'm so chauvinistic, I even root for New York to raise more money than Los Angeles on the Arthritis Telethon. And we usually do.

California: bordering always on the Pacific and sometimes on the ridiculous. So, why do I live here?

Because the sun goes down a block from my house.

SUN OF GOD

I've begun worshipping the sun for a number of reasons. First of all, unlike some other gods I could mention, I can see the sun. It's there for me every day. And the things it brings me are quite apparent all the time: heat, light, food, a lovely day. There's no mystery, no one asks for money, I don't have to dress up, and there's no boring pageantry. And interestingly enough, I have found that the prayers I offer to the sun and the prayers I formerly offered to "God" are all answered at about the same 50-percent rate.

SMALL TOWNS
You know you're in a small town when:

{ } The restaurant closes at lunch so the waitress can go home and eat.

{ } The mayor's nickname is "Greasy Dick" and besides appearing on the ballot, it also appears on his driver's license.

✖ The fashion boutique/post office is located in one corner of the hardware store between the used milking machines and the pay toilet.

{ } The police station is closed evenings and weekends, but they leave lit the sign that gives the time and temperature.

{ } The newspaper prints the crossword puzzle on the front page above the fold, and prints the answers just below.

{ } The zip code has three digits and features a decimal point.

{ } The Narcotics Anonymous chapter has only one member, and he's strung out on ranch dressing.

A NAME BY ANY OTHER NAME

Whatever happened to Eddie? Where did he go? Seems like he was just here. And where's Billy? And Bobby and Jackie and John? Jimmy, Paul, Vinny, Tom, and Charlie? And Richie? Where did they go?

And where the fuck did Cameron come from? And Jordan and Justin and Shane and Parker? Tucker, Tyler, Taylor, Carter, Flynn, Blake, and Cody? Who let these people in? Brett? Brent? Blair? Cassidy? Where are all these goofy names coming from? Say what you will about the national candidates in 1996, at least they had the decency to be named Bill, Bob, Al, and Jack.

The popularity of first names is perishable; they pass in and out of favor. Occasionally, newspapers will print the most popular names given to babies that year, and they're never the same as years before. You don't run into many little girls named Bertha or Edith. Nor are there a lot of Netties, Effies, Opals, Hopes, or Pearls floatin' around the day care. Ditto Ethel, Nellie, Myrtle, Agatha, and Mabel. And how many expectant parents are praying for a girl so they can name her Blanche, Clara, Agnes, or Lottie? None. You know why? Because most of those women are in nursing homes.

But thanks to the "trendies"—and the sheer passage of time—someday our substandard nursing homes will be filled with Ambers, Kaylas, Tiffanys, Caitlins, Morgans, Courtneys, Whitneys, Cheyennes, Ashleys, Megans, Brittanys, and Heathers. And that's not to overlook Judi, Lori, Suzi, Debi, Keli, and Wendi, and any other name that can conceiveably be spelled with a final "i."

There are even some girls whose names don't end in "y" who can't resist that trend: "Hi, my name is Margaret, but somehow, I spell it with an 'i.'"

There are women named Faith, Hope, Joy, and Prudence. Why not Despair, Guilt, Rage, and Grief? It seems only right. "Tom, I'd like you to meet the girl of my dreams, Tragedy." These days, Trajedi.

I had an uncle who was embarassed because he had a

woman's name. We told him not to worry, lots of men have women's names: Leslie, Marion, Chris, Dale, Lonnie. We tried to reassure him. But old Uncle Margaret Mary . . . I guess he just couldn't handle it. I don't know why, it never bothered his wife, Turk.

Do you know why hurricanes have names instead of numbers? To keep the killing personal. No one cares about a bunch of people killed by a number. "200 Dead as Number Three Slams Ashore" is not nearly as interesting a headline as "Charlie Kills 200." Death is much more satisfying and entertaining if you personalize it.

Me, I'm still waitin' for Hurricane Ed. Old Ed wouldn't hurt ya, would he? Sounds kinda friendly. "Hell no, we ain't evacuatin'. Ed's comin'!"

Guess the white guy: Odell, Tyrone, Tremaine, and Sparky. Guess the black girl: Cathy, Joan, Peggy, and Vondella.

First names can even suggest how tough you are. Who would you want on your side in a bar fight? Arnold, Seymour, Jasper, and Percy? Or Nitro, Hacksaw, Rhino, and Skull?

And, guys, which women would you rather run into when you're out drinking: Lillian, Priscilla, and Judith? Or Trixie, Bubbles, and Candy?

The Kennedy family changed William Kennedy Smith's first name in order to influence the outcome of his rape trial. They changed it from Willie to Will because guys named Will hardly ever go to jail, while America's prisons are chock full of Willies. Will is all-American, Willie is . . . well, just ask Michael Dukakis.

Through all these years, I have kept alive my one remaining childhood Catholic fantasy: I'm hoping that someday a new pope will choose the name Corky. Just once in my life, I want to look up at that balcony and see His Holiness, Pope Corky IX. I think you'd have to skip straight to nine to give him a little credibility, don't you? Somehow, Pope Corky the First doesn't command a great deal of authority.

That's because some names are inappropriate in the wrong settings. You won't find many Schuyler Vanderpools blowin' into a harmonica on death row; no one in need of brain surgery is breakin' down the door to see Dr. Lucky Lipshitz; and I'm sure only the most devoted aficionado would pay money to see a ballet dancer named Bruno McNulty.

On the other hand, you'll know that America has relaxed its hopelessly tight asshole if we someday elect a president named Booger. If we ever get a president named Booger, Skeeter, T-Bone, or Downtown President Brown, you'll know that finally this country is a relaxed, comfortable place to live.

The point is, there are emotional values that attach to names; they carry psychological baggage. Just think of the Old West. I'm sure if Billy the Kid's name had been Billy the Schmuck, people wouldn't have been afraid.

"Who's that ridin' into town?"

"Billy the Schmuck."

"Oh. Well, fuck 'im!"

Would anyone have paid to see a Wild West show if the star attraction was Buffalo Shecky?

Using this approach, western movies would have been completely unbelievable:

"Hey, Shemp! Go get Sheriff Quackenbush, there's gonna be trouble. Two-Gun Noodleman and Wild Bill Swackhammer are drunk, and they're lookin' for Deadeye Stoopnagle."

This also applies to the legendary criminals of the thirties. Do you think the police would've spent a lot of time looking for Pretty Boy Heffleflekker?

And what about Jack the Ripper? If his name had been Wally, I don't think people would have been afraid to walk the streets of London. Not if they thought Wally the Ripper was on the loose.

"Who's that? Wally who? Wally the Ripper? Ha-ha-ha-ha! Really? Wally the Ripper, indeed! Ha-ha-ha-ha!"

Religion presents an interesting situation. Jerry Falwell; it's simply an absurd name for a clergyman. The last person in the world I'm going to believe has an inside track with God is some guy named Jerry. Can you imagine the supreme being, in the middle of the night, "Jerry! Wake up. I got some revelations."

On the other hand, the founders of the major religions had names that seem quite suitable. There's still a certain mystery surrounding the names Buddha, Moses, and Mohammed. But the poor Mormons. All they could come up with was Joseph Smith. Not too impressive.

"Listen, Caleb, we got a new religion. You wanna join?"

"Who started it?"

"Joe Smith."

"See ya later."

You can't blame him. I wouldn't follow a guy named Joe Smith halfway across a continent, either.

"C'mon, we're goin' to Utah."

"Why?"

"Joe Smith said that's where we're supposed to be."

"Well, I'm gonna finish this crossword. Why don'tcha drop me a postcard."

In ancient times, the rulers had magnificent names: Alexander the Great. Suppose he had been a less imposing figure, do you think he would have been called Alexander the Marginal? As it is, he had his detractors. You know, people who called him Alexander the Scumbag.

History has given us other impressive names from simpler times: Edward the Fair, Charles the Bold, Catherine the Great. These days, they would be Edward the Abuse Victim, Charles the Underachiever, and Catherine the Recovering Codependent.

And let's not forget the historical figures we never hear of: Tiberius the Wanker and Lucretius the Dog Fucker. Guys like that.

And I'm sure history would not be the same if certain names had been slightly different. For example, World War II would have ended much more quickly if we had been fighting a guy named Skip Hitler.

Suppose there had been a really outstanding eighteenth-century composer who was better than Beethoven, Bach, and Mozart combined. But his name was Joey the Cocksucker. Do you think he would be famous today? "And now, Eugene Ormandy conducts the Philadelphia Orchestra as they perform the Requiem Mass in C-sharp Minor, composed by Joey the Cocksucker."

Some names are embarrassing. We had a guy in our neighborhood, Michael Hunt, who called himself Mickey because the only alternative was Mike Hunt. Of course, some other names are just plain dirty: "Hi, I'm Peter Ball, and this is Dick Cox. We're friends of Randy Bush."

Some people have funny names. They can't help it, but it's hard to keep from laughing when a guy named Elmo Zipaloonie introduces you to his friend El Cunto Prickolini. And if you want funny, you can't beat farmers with names like Orville Pigdicker and Hooter Stumpfuck.

Speaking of funny names, do you realize Howdy Doody's mother and father are known as the Doodys? And Bo Diddley's parents are the Diddleys? How would you like to be at a party and have to introduce the Doodys to the Diddleys? And keep a straight face? "Mr. and Mrs. Doody, I'd like you to meet Mr. and Mrs. Diddley. Mr. Doody, Mr. Diddley; Mrs. Diddley, Mrs. Doody. Mr. Doody, Mrs. Diddley; Mr. Diddley, Mrs. Doody. The Doodys, the Diddleys; the Diddleys, the Doodys." Jesus!

Then, just as you finish all of that, in walks Bo Diddley's brother, Dudley Diddley, and his sisters, Dottie Diddley, Dodie Diddley, and Didi Diddley. And Howdy Doody's sisters, Judy Doody and Trudy Doody. I'd never get through it all. I'd be leanin' over the punchbowl, thinkin', "Please, God, don't let Rootie Kazootie show up."

In Hawaii, I once had the pleasure of meeting Don Ho and his lovely wife, Heidi. Plus his three brothers, Gung, Land, and Hy.

Hospitals often name a new facility after the person who makes the major donation. I grew up with a neighborhood guy who is now extremely wealthy, and I'm hoping someday he'll make a big donation. I just wanna drive past the hospital and see the "No-Balls" Malone Cancer Pavilion.

I've noticed there are a lot of people named Rice, but no one seems to be named Corn.

The artist currently known as The Artist Formerly Known as Prince was presumably trying to shorten his name when he changed it from Prince to an unpronounceable symbol. It didn't work. His name is now five times longer than it was before.

They have Walnut Street and Chestnut Street, but you know what they don't have? Peanut Street. What's wrong with that? And how about some other nuts? Wouldn't you like to live on Pistachio Place? Or Cashew Boulevard? How about a nice big house out on Dry-Roasted Mixed Nuts Lane?

If they have a shoe store called Athlete's Foot, why can't they have a hat store called Ringworm?

There's a planet named Pluto, but we don't have one named Goofy. Goofy would be a good name for this planet. It certainly qualifies.

Just to put a button on this topic: It is said that Indians were sometimes named for the first thing they saw when they were born. Makes you wonder why there aren't more Indians named Hairy Pussy, doesn't it?

And, as Baretta used to say, that's the name of that tune.

THINGS YOU NEVER SEE

{ } A puppet with a hard-on

{ } A butterfly with a swastika design

{ } The Latin word for *douche bag*

{ } Someone defecating in church

{ } A junkie with leisure time

{ } A serial killer with a light-up bow tie

{ } A mom-and-pop steel mill

{ } A shot glass full of carrot juice

{ } A bum with matching luggage

{ } Really interesting twins

{ } Condoms with pictures of the saints

{ } Two homosexuals who own a bait shop

{ } A pimp with a low profit margin

{ } A Rolls-Royce that's more than 50 percent primer paint

IT'S YOUR BODY: FEARLESS FASHIONS

I like to look at tattoos on people; I think they're cool. But I would never get one. I always thought it was a bad idea to let some guy draw a picture on me that'll probably never come off. Ya know? I'm conservative on this one. Not only the thing never comes off, but it hurts to put it on, and you gotta pay the guy. Plus if you *do* wanna take it off, it hurts again, and you gotta pay the guy again.

Another reason not to get a tattoo is that a tattoo is positive identification. No one should ever do anything to help the police. In any way. Especially when you may be the object of their interest.

So I never got a tattoo. But I had some good ideas. I was gonna get dotted lines tattooed on all my joints, wherever I bend. With little instructions: "Fold here." "Do not glue."

I also thought about gettin' a necklace of hickeys.

Here's one I almost went through with. I was gonna get my nipples tattooed as radio dials: "volume" and "tuning." And the hair in the middle of my chest was gonna be the speaker. For stereo, I'd raise my arms. Armpit speakers!

I guess the most popular tattoo of all time is MOM. A lot of guys get MOM. No one ever gets POP. You know why? Cause you can't read POP in the mirror. In a mirror, MOM comes out MOM. POP comes out "909." What the fuck is that?

If you guys want to get a MOM tattoo and save a little money, just get two letters done. Get about a one-inch capital *M* tattooed on each cheek of your ass in pink and brown ink. Then when you bend over, it says "Mom." Also, later on if you're havin' sex with your girlfriend, and her parents are in the next room, when you finish up you can just lie on your back, draw your legs up to your chest and silently say, "Wow!"

Here's another good one for guys: at the top of your inner thigh, next to your groin, you put, "In case of emergency, pull handle." Or get your penis tattooed to resemble a candy cane. Great for Christmas blow jobs. But be very careful not to let the tattoo guy bend your penis into a *J* shape.

Get the words, "tote bag" tattooed on your scrotum. Or "Bloomingdale's" might be good. "Cartier" would be more appropriate; a little hairy pouch for your precious jewels.

How about a tattoo of the Three Stooges peering into your asshole? Or a serpent coming out? Or a nice tattoo of Madonna with her hand up your ass? Here's a good one for right next to your asshole: "No gerbils!" Or, "Gerbils welcome." Depending on what puts a smile on your face.

Here would be a great tattoo for right in the middle of your forehead: "I have colored ink in my skin!" Or, "Your message here. Fifty cents." How about, "Yeah, it's a tattoo, you miserable prick! Right in the middle of my forehead. If you don't like it, suck my dick!" This will really keep you from having to deal with that bothersome job market.

And here's a solution to an age old tattoo problem. If your girlfriend's name, say, "Suzie," is tattooed on your arm, and you break up with her, don't have the tattoo removed. Just have the tattoo reworked so it says, "Fuck Suzie."

By the way, you don't actually have to do all these things; they're just suggestions. Think them over first. Sit down, have six or seven vodkas, and give them a few seconds thought.

Besides, you wanna know something? Tattoos are passé. They're yesterday's thing. I'm lookin' for the *next* big thing in body decoration. And I think I may have it.

Everyone's skin has imperfections. It's unavoidable. Pockmarks, wrinkles, bullet holes, scars, blotches, stab wounds, cysts, warts, needle holes, acne pits, enlarged pores.

I think people should see these imperfections and disfigurements as positive things. Flaws and defects can actually be forms of decoration.

Take moles, God's punctuation marks. Moles are great, and they can be useful if you want a really interesting look. The only problem is they're usually randomly placed; they don't represent anything. I think plastic surgeons should offer a new service: rearranging people's moles. Think of your moles as fashion accessories. "God, look at all the moles that guy has!" "Yes, and aren't they nicely arranged?"

There are lots of things you can do with moles: make the double helix, do a happy Hitler face, spell out the name of your bowling team. And how about moles with velcro, so you could change your look every day? Here's something novel. Choose a good size mole on your arm, and tattoo little legs sticking out of the sides. People will constantly be trying to shoo the "bug" off your arm. It's great for picking up girls.

Next, body-piercing. Now, the piercing movement is off to a good start, and I like the idea behind it: self-esteem through self-mutiliation. I've always said, when in doubt, punch a hole in yourself. That's fine, but I think the piercing people are missing a good bet. Vital organs. I mean, skin is one thing. That's easy. But how about getting your lungs or kidneys pierced? Why not some lovely diamond studs all over the surface of your liver? Or a couple of nice 18-karat gold rings hanging from your thyroid gland?

But, you know, stuff like this might not be dangerous enough for today's happenin' people. What's really gonna be great is when the ozone layer is completely gone, and everyone has melanomas. Then you'll start to see "fashion skin cancer." It'll probably start in Malibu. People will use their skin cancers to form little designs. Since it's Malibu, a lot of them will do their zodiac sign. Of course, if your sign is Cancer, you'll be in real good shape.

I believe skin cancer will eventually become part of every American's fashion arsenal. "That's a lovely growth, Bambi. Twenty millimeters and right between your eyes. God, I'm so jealous!"

Before I leave this subject, I have two more ideas for the truly avant garde: How about living small, live mammals medically grafted onto your skin? Wouldn't you like to have a prairie dog living in the middle of your chest, sharing your blood supply? How about an adult male Norwegian rat sewn onto the top of your head, keeping an eye on everything?

I think we also might take a page from Africa's book and get into deliberate scarring. Not ritual scars that form coherent designs. Random scarring! Let a bunch of drunks with swords inflict hundreds of small, deep cuts on your skin. Or have a friend throw boiling grease all over you, then sit back and see what develops.

I don't believe the body-decorating trend has reached its peak yet, and as it does, I shall try to be at the forefront, always pointing America toward the hot new look.

SHINE ON

I'm glad sunscreen has been shown to be associated with more skin cancer rather than less. It's not in the mainstream media yet, but the biggest jump in skin cancer has occurred since the advent of sunscreens. That kind of thing makes me happy. The fact that people, in pursuit of a superficial look of health, give themselves a fatal disease. I love it when "reasoning" human beings think they have figured out how to beat something and it comes right back and kicks them in the nuts. God bless the law of unintended consequences. And the irony is impressive: Healthy people, trying to look healthier, make themselves sick. Good!

COOLEST T-SHIRT

I finally escaped what I think of as the "Coolest T-shirt Trap." I realized that no matter how cool I think my T-shirt is, no one else is gonna think so, because everybody thinks *they* have the coolest T-shirt.

There are times when you take fifteen minutes to pick out which shirt to wear, because you're going to a place where there'll be a bunch of guys you've never met; guys you might even secretly want to impress. So you settle on that special black, limited-edition number that your brother brought back from the Middle East. The one that shows Saddam Hussein peeking out of a garbage can, flashing his middle finger and saying, "Ha ha, Mister Bush, you missed me. I was here at home all the time." And you think, "No one has ever seen a shirt like this; this will make them jealous. They'll all want it and wonder where I got it. I'll definitely have the coolest T-shirt."

And then when you get there, no one cares at all. No one even tries to read the writing. And all the other guys turn out to be dorks who will wear any piece of shit that's handed to them. Like "Property of Alcatraz," "No Fear," "Gold's Gym," and "Life Is a Beach." What a letdown.

Personally I haven't worn T-shirts with writing on them for about ten years, but I do own what I consider to be the coolest T-shirt in the world. It's plain white, and inside a kind of faded maroon circle, in an odd, feminine sort of print, it says, "Fuck the Cows." But it's about two sizes too small. Ain't that always the way?

TALKING AND LISTENING

You know how sometimes, at a busy cocktail party, when you're telling a group of people a story, a few of them may become distracted, and you lose their attention? So you concentrate a little harder on the ones who are still listening? You know that feeling? And then, because it's a lively party, a few more of them drift away? And as your audience slowly peels off one by one, after a while you wind up addressing any person you can find who's willing look at you. Even the busboy. And then you realize the busboy doesn't understand English. Isn't that awful?

Sometimes, a person some distance away from you will say something you can't quite understand, so you ask them to repeat it, and you still can't make it out. You try two or three more times without any luck, and by then you're getting embarrassed, so you pretend to understand, and just say, "Yeah!" so you can be done with it. Later, it turns out they said, "We're coming over tonight to remove your wife's ovaries. Will that be all right?"

I CAN'T RECALL

One recent morning there was something I couldn't remember. I sort of knew what it was related to, but I couldn't quite bring it to mind. It seemed like the letter *m* was involved. Then, suddenly, it came to me. That was in the morning. Then, later that afternoon, even though I was able to recall my experience that morning of not being able to remember something, I could no longer remember what the thing was, what it was related to, or what letter of the alphabet had been involved. But what's strange to me is that that morning, the *first* time I couldn't remember it, the thing did eventually come back to me. Later that afternoon, however, in spite of my earlier success, I drew a complete blank. I still don't know what it was, and the nice thing is that a month from now I will have no memory of the incident what-soever. Unless, of course, something reminds me of it.

A PLACE FOR YOUR STUFF

Hi! How are ya? You got your stuff with you? I'll bet you do. Guys have stuff in their pockets; women have stuff in their purses. Of course, some women have pockets, and some guys have purses. That's okay. There's all different ways of carryin' your stuff.

Then there's all the stuff you have in your car. You got stuff in the trunk. Lotta different stuff: spare tire, jack, tools, old blanket, extra pair of sneakers. Just in case you wind up barefoot on the highway some night.

And you've got other stuff in your car. In the glove box. Stuff you might need in a hurry: flashlight, map, sunglasses, automatic weapon. You know. Just in case you wind up bare-foot on the highway some night.

So stuff is important. You gotta take care of your stuff. You gotta have a *place* for your stuff. Everybody's gotta have a place for their stuff. That's what life is all about, tryin' to find a place for your stuff! That's all your house is: a place to keep your stuff. If you didn't have so much stuff, you wouldn't *need* a house. You could just walk around all the time.

A house is just a pile of stuff with a cover on it. You can see that when you're taking off in an airplane. You look down and see all the little piles of stuff. Everybody's got his own little pile of stuff. And they lock it up! That's right! When you leave your house, you gotta lock it up. Wouldn't want somebody to come by and *take* some of your stuff. 'Cause they always take the *good* stuff! They don't bother with that crap you're saving. Ain't nobody interested in your fourth-grade arithmetic papers. *National Geographics*, commemorative plates, your prize collection of Navajo underwear; they're not interested. They just want the good stuff; the shiny stuff; the electronic stuff.

So when you get right down to it, your house is nothing more than a place to keep your stuff . . . while you go out and get . . . *more stuff.* 'Cause that's what this country is all about. Tryin' to get more stuff. Stuff you don't want, stuff you don't need, stuff that's poorly made, stuff that's overpriced. Even stuff you can't afford! Gotta keep on gettin' more stuff. Otherwise someone else might wind up with more stuff. Can't let that happen. Gotta have the most stuff.

So you keep gettin' more and more stuff, and puttin' it in different places. In the closets, in the attic, in the basement, in the garage. And there might even be some stuff you left at your parents' house: baseball cards, comic books, photographs, souvenirs. Actually, your parents threw that stuff out long ago.

So now you got a houseful of stuff. And, even though you might like your house, you gotta move. Gotta get a bigger house. Why? Too much stuff! And that means you gotta move all your stuff. Or maybe, put some of your stuff in storage. Storage! Imagine that. There's a whole industry based on keepin' an eye on other people's stuff.

Or maybe you could sell some of your stuff. Have a yard sale, have a garage sale! Some people drive around all weekend just lookin' for garage sales. They don't have enough of their own stuff, they wanna buy other people's stuff.

Or you could take your stuff to the swap meet, the flea market, the rummage sale, or the auction. There's a lotta ways to get rid of stuff. You can even give your stuff away. The Salvation Army and Goodwill will actually come to your house and pick up your stuff and give it to people who don't have much stuff. It's part of what economists call the Redistribution of Stuff.

OK, enough about your stuff. Let's talk about other people's stuff. Have you ever noticed when you visit someone else's house, you never quite feel at home? You know why? No room for your stuff! Somebody *else's* stuff is all over the place. And what crummy stuff it is! "God! Where'd they get *this* stuff?"

And you know how sometimes when you're visiting someone, you unexpectedly have to stay overnight? It gets real late, and you decide to stay over? So they put you in a bedroom they don't use too often . . . because Grandma died in it eleven years ago! And they haven't moved any of her stuff? Not even the vaporizer?

Or whatever room they put you in, there's usually a dresser or a nightstand, and there's never any room on it for your stuff. Someone else's shit is on the dresser! Have you noticed that their stuff is shit, and your shit is stuff? "Get this shit off of here, so I can put my stuff down!" Crap is also a form of stuff. Crap is the stuff that belongs to the person you just broke up with. "When are you comin' over here to pick up the rest of your crap?"

Now, let's talk about traveling. Sometimes you go on vacation, and you gotta take some of your stuff. Mostly stuff to wear. But which stuff should you take? Can't take all your stuff. Just the stuff you really like; the stuff that fits you well that month. In effect, on vacation, you take a smaller, "second version" of your stuff.

Let's say you go to Honolulu for two weeks. You gotta take two big suitcases of stuff. Two weeks, two big suitcases. That's the stuff you check onto the plane. But you also got your carry-on stuff, plus the stuff you bought in the airport. So now you're all set to go. You got stuff in the overhead rack, stuff under the seat, stuff in the seat pocket, and stuff in your lap. And let's not forget the stuff you're gonna steal from the airline: silverware, soap, blanket, toilet paper, salt and pepper shakers. Too bad those headsets won't work at home.

And so you fly to Honolulu, and you claim your stuff— if the airline didn't drop it in the ocean—and you go to the hotel, and the first thing you do is put away your stuff. There's lots of places in a hotel to put your stuff.

"I'll put some stuff in here, you put some stuff in there. Hey, don't put your stuff in *there*! That's my stuff! Here's another place! Put some stuff in here. And there's another place! Hey, you know what? We've got more places than we've got stuff! We're gonna hafta go out and buy . . . *more stuff!!!*"

Finally you put away all your stuff, but you don't quite feel at ease, because you're a long way from home. Still, you sense that you must be OK, because you do have some of your stuff with you. And so you relax in Honolulu on that basis. That's when your friend from Maui calls and says, "Hey, why don't you come over to Maui for the weekend and spend a couple of nights over here?"

Oh no! Now whaddya bring? Can't bring all this stuff. You gotta bring an even *smaller* version of your stuff. Just enough stuff for a weekend on Maui. The "third version" of your stuff.

And, as you're flyin' over to Maui, you realize that you're really spread out now: You've got stuff all over the world!! Stuff at home, stuff in the garage, stuff at your parents' house (maybe), stuff in storage, stuff in Honolulu, and stuff on the plane. Supply lines are getting longer and harder to maintain!

Finally you get to your friends' place on Maui, and they give you a little room to sleep in, and there's a nightstand. Not much room on it for your stuff, but it's OK because you don't have much stuff now. You got your 8 x 10 autographed picture of Drew Carey, a large can of gorgonzola-flavored Cheez Whiz, a small, unopened packet of brown confetti, a relief map of Corsica, and a family-size jar of peppermint-flavored, petrified egg whites. And you know that even though you're a long way from home, you must be OK because you do have a good supply of peppermint-flavored, petrified egg whites. And so you begin to relax in Maui on that basis. That's when your friend says, "Hey, I think tonight we'll go over to the other side of the island and visit my sister. Maybe spend the night over there."

Oh no! Now whaddya bring? Right! You gotta bring an even smaller version. The "fourth version" of your stuff. Just the stuff you *know* you're gonna need: Money, keys, comb, wallet, lighter, hankie, pen, cigarettes, contraceptives, Vaseline, whips, chains, whistles, dildos, and a book. Just the stuff you *hope* you're gonna need. Actually, your friend's sister probably has her own dildos.

By the way, if you go to the beach while you're visiting the sister, you're gonna have to bring—that's right—an even smaller version of your stuff: the "fifth version." Cigarettes and wallet. That's it. You can always borrow someone's suntan lotion. And then suppose, while you're there on the beach, you decide to walk over to the refreshment stand to get a hot dog? That's right, my friend! Number six! The most important version of your stuff: your wallet! Your wallet contains the only stuff you really can't do without.

Well, by the time you get home you're pretty fed up with your stuff and all the problems it creates. And so about a week later, you clean out the closet, the attic, the basement, the garage, the storage locker, and all the other places you keep your stuff, and you get things down to manageable proportions. Just the right amount of stuff to lead a simple and uncomplicated life. And that's when the phone rings. It's a lawyer. It seems your aunt has died . . . and left you all her stuff. Oh no! Now whaddya do? Right. You do the only thing you can do. The honorable thing. You tell the lawyer to stuff it.

AIR POLLUTION

Think of how much information, in the form of radio energy, there is flying through the air, all around us, all over the world, right now and all the time. AM, FM, UHF, VHF, shortwave radio, television, CB radio, walkie-talkies, cell phones, cordless phones, telephone satellites, microwave relays, faxes, pagers, taxi calls, police, sheriff, hospitals, fire departments, telemetry, navigation, radar, the military, government, financial, legal, medical, the media, etc., etc., etc. Trillions and trillions and trillions and trillions of separate little bits of electronic information flying all around the world through the air at all times. Think of that. Think of how busy the air is. Now realize this: A hundred years ago there was none. None. Silence.

MENTAL BRAIN THOUGHTS

These are the things I think about when I'm sitting home alone and the power goes out:

If something in the future is canceled, what is canceled? What has really happened? Something that didn't occur yet is now never going to occur at all. Does that qualify as an event?

There's a place you've never seen, but for many years you've pictured it in your mind. Then you finally see it. After you leave, do you continue to picture it the old way?

Imagine a place called Moravia; a nonexistent country. See it in your mind. See a few details. OK, now Moravia ceases to exist. Is your picture of the original, nonexistent country different from what it looks like now that it ceases to exist? Why? They're both nonexistent.

OK, picture Moravia again, the original way. Now Moravia is invaded by a neighboring country, Boronia. Picture Boronia. It's completely different from Moravia. Different geography, different ethnic stock, beliefs, way of life, government, everything. See it? Anyway, Boronia invades Moravia and occupies it, and begins to make some changes. Now picture Moravia again. Does it look different? Isn't that weird? It looks a little like Boronia.

Here's another one. You've never been to your friend's place of work, but you've pictured it. Then he changes jobs, but it's a similar job. Do you bother to change your mental picture of where he works? By how much?

Or your friend works at one Wendy's and gets transferred to a different Wendy's. Do you picture a whole new Wendy's? Or do you get lazy and say, "They're all pretty much the same, so I'll just go with the old one."

If a radio station changes its call letters, moves its studio across town, hires all new disk jockeys, and changes the style of music it plays, but keeps the same frequency, is it still the same radio station? Suppose they change only the music?

On a given day, Flight 23 goes from New York to Los Angeles. The following month, Flight 23 goes from New York to Los Angeles again, but the crew is different, the passengers are different and it's a completely different airplane. How can both flights be Flight 23? They can't.

A week has no basis in nature as do days, months, and years. So, birds don't understand weeks or weekdays. They do know enough to come back to the sidewalk café every day for crumbs. But suppose the café is in the business district and closed on weekends? What do the birds think of that? I'll bet they're really glad when Monday rolls around. Unlike the rest of us.

These are just a few of the thoughts that kept me out of the really good schools.

THE GEORGE CARLIN BOOK CLUB— "We've Got Books Out the Ass"
Offer #1: "How-To" Titles

❪ ❫ *How to Remove Chewing Gum from Your Bush*

❪ ❫ *How to Turn Your Front Lawn into a Cathouse*

❪ ❫ *How to Remove an Infected Cyst from a Loved One*

❪ ❫ *How to Make Two Small Hats out of a Brassiere*

❪ ❫ *How to Make a Brassiere out of Two Small Hats*

❪ ❫ *How to Have Really Nice Lymph Glands*

✖ *How to Act Laid-Back During a Grease Fire*

❪❫ *How to Spot a Creep from Across the Street*

❪❫ *How to Dance with a Swedish Person*

❪❫ *How to Induce a Clergyman to Grab You by the Nuts*

❪❫ *How to Milk a Dog While It's Sleeping*

❪❫ *How to Get Through College without Books*

❪❫ *How to Make a Small Salad out of Your Work Pants*

✖ *How to Lure a Weasel into a Cardboard Box*

❪❫ *How to Filet a Panda*

❪❫ *How to Get a Tan with a Blow Torch*

❪❫ *How to Make an Oil Lamp out of Your Genitals*

✖ *How to Style Your Hair with a Bullwhip*

❪❫ *How to Convert an Old Leather Chair into Twelve Pairs of Shoes*

❪❫ *How to Achieve Multiple Orgasms with a Pair of Tweezers*

❪❫ *How to Kill a Rat with a Paper Clip*

❪❫ *How to Lease Out the Space Inside Your Nose*

❪❫ *How to Spot Truly Vicious People in Church*

✖ *How to Become a Total Fuckin' Greaseball*

NO ONE EVER WROTE THIS SENTENCE BEFORE

On the Feast of St. Stephen, I was driving my hearse to the wholesale liverwurst outlet when suddenly a hermaphrodite in a piano truck backed out of a crackhouse driveway, and, as my shoes caught fire, I pirouetted across Boris Karloff Boulevard, slapping the truckdriver six times in the loins with a Chattanooga road map, even though he was humming "The Pussycat Song."

Z-Z-Z-Z-Z-Z-Z-Z-Z-Z

People say, "I'm going to sleep now," as if it were nothing. But it's really a bizarre activity. "For the next several hours, while the sun is gone, I'm going to become unconscious, temporarily losing command over everything I know and understand. When the sun returns, I will resume my life."

If you didn't know what sleep was, and you had only seen it in a science fiction movie, you would think it was weird and tell all your friends about the movie you'd seen.

"They had these people, you know? And they would walk around all day and be OK? And then, once a day, usually after dark, they would lie down on these special platforms and become unconscious. They would stop functioning almost completely, except deep in their minds they would have adventures and experiences that were completely impossible in real life. As they lay there, completely vulnerable to their enemies, their only movements were to occasionally shift from one position to another; or, if one of the 'mind adventures' got too real, they would sit up and scream and be glad they weren't unconscious anymore. Then they would drink a lot of coffee."

So, next time you see someone sleeping, make believe you're in a science fiction movie. And whisper, "The creature is regenerating itself."

FUCK THE FARMERS

Can someone please tell me why farmers are always whining and looking for a handout? If it isn't a drought or a flood, it's their bad loans. I was always told farmers were strong, independent people who were too proud to accept help. But sure enough as soon as something goes wrong, they're looking for the government to bail them out. And they're the first ones to complain about city people who live on welfare. Fuck the farmers. They're worrying about losing their land? It wasn't their land to begin with, they stole it from the Indians. Let 'em find out what it feels like to have your land taken away by some square-headed cocksucker who just came over on a boat. They wiped out the bears, the wolves, and the mountain lions; they spoiled the land, poisoned the water table, and they produce tasteless food. Why is it in this capitalist society all businesses are expected to succeed or fail on their own except farming? Why is that?

SMOKE IF YA GOT 'EM

Even though I don't smoke, I'm not one of those fanatics you run into. In fact, I love watching cigarette smokers in their sad little sealed-off areas, sucking away, deep lines in their faces, precancerous lesions taking hold, the posture and body language of petty criminals. You know what you do with these people? Give 'em free cigarettes. Let 'em smoke. Offer them a light! And you hope each one of them gets a small, painful tumor right in the middle of his body so it can grow in six different directions at once. And you pray they get a doctor who doesn't believe in painkillers, and their insurance runs out. I think people should be allowed to enjoy themselves.

BLAME IT ON THE BOSSA NOVA

They try to blame movies and TV for violence in this country. What a load of shit. Long before there were movies and television, Americans killed millions of Indians, enslaved millions of blacks, slaughtered 700,000 of each other in a family feud, and attained the highest murder rate in history. Don't blame Sylvester Stallone. We brought these horrifying genes with us from Europe, and then we gave them our own special twist. American know-how!

Violent American movies like *Die Hard*, *Terminator*, and *Lethal Weapon* do very well in places like Canada, Japan, and Europe. Very well. Yet these countries do not have nearly the violence of the United States. In 1989, in all of Japan, with a population of 150 million, there were 754 murders. In New York City that year, with a population of only 7.5 million, there were 2,300. It's bred in the bone. Movies and television don't make you violent; all they do is channel the violence more creatively.

Americans even manage to turn positive experiences into violence. Like sports championships. In Detroit, in 1990, the Pistons won the NBA championship: eight people dead. The Chicago Bulls, 1993: nine shot, 1,000 arrested. Montreal, the Canadiens, 1993: 170 injured, 47 police cars vandalized, and $10 million in damages. I'm glad it's happened in a place like Montreal, so these bigoted shit stains who call in on sports-talk shows can't blame it all on the blacks.

I could mention plenty of things that contribute to violence. One is simply the condition of being violent; the predisposition. Everyone knows this is a cranky species. It's especially well known among the other species. And most people can see that the particular strain of critter found in America is especially prone to graceless outbursts, being, as we are, a collection of all the strange and restless castoffs and rolling stones who proved such an ill fit back home. God bless them all, and give them all the guns they want.

Two other things that contribute to violence are religion and government, because they seek to repress and regulate natural impulses like sex and self-gratification. Of course, the two of them will always try to scapegoat movies and television. The truth is, no one knows enough or cares enough to stop the real violence, so their answer is to tone down the pretend violence. It's superstition: "Maybe if we tone down the pretend violence, the real violence will go away. Or not seem so bad."

And maybe the father who forbids his son to watch violent television will not beat the shit out of him when he disobeys.

Maybe.

"HI MOM!"

A man is seated in a football stadium with a small TV set tuned to the game. The sideline camera takes his picture, and his image travels through the lens, out of the camera, to the truck, to the satellite, to a ground station several miles away, back into the air, and to the man's TV set.

He sees himself on the screen. The image travels from his eyes to his brain. His brain sends a signal to his arm to start waving. The image travels to the camera, through the lens, to the truck, to the satellite, to another ground station a thousand miles away where it is retransmitted into the air and picked up by a cable company that sends it to the man's parents' TV set.

The image travels from the screen to his mother's eyes, along the optic nerve to her brain, where it references her memory and recognition takes place. Her brain then sends a series of signals to her lungs, throat, lips, and tongue, and she says, "Look, it's Mike!"

BASEBALL AND FOOTBALL

Baseball is different from any other sport; very different.

For instance, in most sports you score points or goals; in baseball you score runs.

In most sports the ball, or object, is put in play by the offensive team; in baseball the defensive team puts the ball in play, and only the defense is allowed to touch the ball. In fact, in baseball if an offensive player touches the ball intentionally, he's out; sometimes unintentionally, he's out.

Also: In football, basketball, soccer, volleyball, and all sports played with a ball, you score *with* the ball, and without the ball you can't score. In baseball the ball prevents you from scoring.

In most sports the team is run by a coach; in baseball the team is run by a manager; and only in baseball does the manager (or coach) wear the same clothing the players do. If you had ever seen John Madden in his Oakland Raiders football uniform, you would know the reason for this custom.

Now, I've mentioned football. Baseball and football are the two most popular spectator sports in this country. And, as such, it seems they ought to be able to tell us something about ourselves and our values. And maybe how those values have changed over the last 150 years. For those reasons, I enjoy comparing baseball and football:

Baseball is a nineteenth-century pastoral game.
Football is a twentieth-century technological struggle.

Baseball is played on a diamond, in a park. The baseball park!
Football is played on a gridiron, in a stadium, sometimes called Soldier Field or War Memorial Stadium.

Baseball begins in the spring, the season of new life.
Football begins in the fall, when everything is dying.

In football you wear a helmet.
In baseball you wear a cap.

Football is concerned with *downs*. "What down is it?"
Baseball is concerned with *ups*. "Who's up? Are you up? I'm not up! He's up!"

In football you receive a penalty.
In baseball you make an error.

In football the specialist comes in to kick.
In baseball the specialist comes in to relieve somebody.

Football has hitting, clipping, spearing, piling on, personal fouls, late hitting, and unnecessary roughness.
Baseball has the sacrifice.

Football is played in any kind of weather: Rain, snow, sleet, hail, fog . . . can't see the game, don't know if there is a game going on; mud on the field . . . can't read the uniforms, can't read the yard markers, the struggle will continue!

In baseball if it rains, we don't go out to play. "I can't go out! It's raining out!"

Baseball has the seventh-inning stretch.

Football has the two-minute warning.

Baseball has no time limit: "We don't know when it's gonna end!"

Football is rigidly timed, and it will end "even if we have to go to sudden death."

In baseball, during the game, in the stands, there's a kind of picnic feeling. Emotions may run high or low, but there's not that much unpleasantness.

In football, during the game in the stands, you can be sure that at least twenty-seven times you were perfectly capable of taking the life of a fellow human being.

And finally, the objectives of the two games are completely different:

In football the object is for the quarterback, otherwise known as the field general, to be on target with his aerial assault, riddling the defense by hitting his receivers with deadly accuracy in spite of the blitz, even if he has to use the shotgun. With short bullet passes and long bombs, he marches his troops into enemy territory, balancing this aerial assault with a sustained ground attack that punches holes in the forward wall of the enemy's defensive line.

In baseball the object is to go home! And to be safe! "I hope I'll be safe at home!"

ERIN GO FUCK YOURSELF

Being Irish, I guess I should resent the Notre Dame nickname, "The Fighting Irish." After all, how long do you think nicknames like "The Bargaining Jews" or "The Murdering Italians" would last? Only the ironic Irish could be so naively honest. I get the feeling that Notre Dame came real close to naming itself "The Fuckin' Drunken, Thick-skulled, Brawling, Short-dicked Irish."

PLAY BALL!!!

Here's something I don't care about: athlete's families. This is really the bottom of the sports barrel. I'm watchin' a ballgame, and just because some athlete's wife is in the stands, someone thinks they have to put her picture on the screen. And I miss a double steal! Same with a ballplayer's father. Goddamn! "There's his dad, who taught him how to throw the changeup when he was two years old." Fuck him, the sick bastard! His own sports dreams probably crash-landed, so he forced a bunch of shit on his kid, and now the kid's a neurotic athlete. Fuck these athletes' relatives. If they wanna be on TV, let 'em get their own goddamn shows. Let 'em go to cable access.

I also don't care if an athlete's wife had a baby, how she is, how the baby is, how much the baby weighs or what the fuckin' baby's name is. It's got nothin' to do with sports. Leave it out!

And I'm tired of athletes whose children are sick. Healthy men with sick children; how banal. The kid's sick? Talk it over privately. Don't spread it all over television. Have some dignity. And play fuckin' ball!!

Nor do I wanna know about some athlete's crippled little brother or his hemophiliac big sister. The Olympics specialize in this kind of mawkish bullshit. Either his aunt has the clap, or his kid has a forty-pound mole, or his high school buddy overdosed on burritos, etc. Can't sports exist on television without all this embarrassing, maudlin, super-sentimental, tear-jerking bullshit? Keep your personal disasters to yourself, and get in there and score some fuckin' points!

And I don't care for all that middlebrow philosophical bullshit you get from athletes and coaches when someone on the team has a serious illness or dies in an accident. They give you that stuff, "When something like this happens, you realize what's really important. It's only a game." Bullshit! If it's only a game, get the fuck out of the business. You know what's important? The score. Who won. I can get plenty of sad tales somewhere else in this victim-packed society. Fuck all that dewy-eyed sentimental bullshit about people who are sick. And that includes any athlete whose father died a week before the game who says, "This one's for Pop." American bathos. Keep it to yourself. Play ball!

And I shouldn't even have to mention severly injured athletes who are playing on "nothing but heart." Fuck you! Suck it up and get out there, motherfucker.

And they're always tellin' ya that one of these athletes has a tumor. Don't they know that no one gives a fuck? You know when you care about a tumor? When *you* have it! Or someone close to you. Who cares about an athlete? No one cares if a rock star gets a tumor. What's so special about an athlete? By the way, you ever notice you don't hear as much about rock stars getting these tumors as you do about athletes? Maybe the drug life is a little better for us than all that stupid sweaty shit the athletes put themselves through. Just speculating.

And I don't wanna know about sports teams that sew the initials of dead people on their jerseys for one whole season as if it really means something. Leave that mawkish bullshit in the locker room. I don't wanna know who's in mourning. Play ball, you fuckin' grotesque overdeveloped nitwits!

And you can skip tellin' me about the Chevrolet player of the game. A thousand-dollar contribution to a scholarship fund in the athlete's name. Shit. A thousand dollars won't even keep a kid in decent drugs for one semester. Fuck Chevrolet.

And when are they gonna discover that no one cares if an athlete is active in local charities? People don't want to know about some coke-headed, steroid monstrosity who's working to help the National Douche Bag Foundation. Or how much he cares about inner-city kids. Can the cocksucker play ball? Fine. Then suit him up and get him the fuck out there on the field and let him injure someone.

One last thing on this topic. No one, repeat, no one is interested in athletes who can sing or play musical instruments. We already have people to perform these tasks. They're called singers and musicians, and, at last count, it would seem we have quite enough of them. The fact that someone with an IQ triple his age has mastered a few simple chords is unimportant and of monumental disinterest. Play ball!

PASS THE ROLES

I'm surprised that all this shit about role models has persisted as long as it has. Why should a kid need a role model? You know what you tell a kid? "Get the fuck out there, get a job, and make a contribution." Never mind that role model shit. If this country is dependent on things like role models, we're much worse off than I thought.

People say athletes should be role models. I never looked up to an athlete, did you? I liked them. I didn't copy them. Did you ever listen to one of those guys talk? Would you want your kid to turn out like that? Willing to completely subordinate his ego and individuality for the sake of a group whose sole purpose is to compete with other groups? Can't have a mustache? Gotta wear a suit jacket? Shit! If your kid needs a role model and you ain't it, you're both fucked.

SPORTS ROUNDUP

I like sports because I enjoy knowing that many of these macho athletes have to vomit before a big game. Any guy who would take a job where you gotta puke first is my kinda guy.

I read that Monica Seles got stabbed. And although I have nothing against Monica Seles, I'm glad somebody in sports got stabbed. I like the idea of it; it's good entertainment. If we're lucky, it'll spread all through sports. And show business, too! Wouldn't you like to see a guy jump up on stage and stab some famous singer? Especially a real shitty pop singer? Maybe they'll even start stabbing comedians. Fuck it, I'm ready! I never perform without my can of mace. I have a switchblade knife, too. I'll cut your eye out and go right on telling jokes.

In football, I root for the Oakland Raiders because they hire castoffs, outlaws, malcontents, and fuckups, they have lots of penalties, fights, and paybacks, and because Al Davis told the rest of the pig NFL owners to go get fucked. Also, they don't have a lot of Christians kneeling down to pray after touchdowns. Christians are ruining sports. Someday, the Raiders will be strong again, and they will dip the ball in shit and shove it down the throats of the wholesome, white, heartland teams that pray together and don't deliver late hits.

You know the best thing I did for myself during the past five years? I told sports to go take a flying fuck. I was fed up with the way I related to professional sports, so I reordered the relationship on my own terms. I became a little more selective.

I couldn't believe how much time I had wasted watching any old piece of shit ballgame that happened to show up on TV. I must have thought there was some inborn male obligation to tune in and root every time a bunch of sweaty assholes got together to mix it up in a stadium somewhere.

I also realized I was wasting perfectly good emotional energy by sticking with my teams when they were doing poorly. My rooting life was scarcely better than those Cubs fans who think it's a sign of character to feel shitty all the time. It's absurd.

I decided it's not necessary to suffer and feel crappy just because my teams suck. What I do now is cut 'em loose for awhile. I simply let them go about losing, as I go about living my life. Then, when they've improved, and are doing well once again, I get back on board and enjoy their success.

Yeah, I know, I can hear it: diehard, asshole loyal sports fans screaming, "Front-runner!" Goddamn right! Don't be so fuckin' juvenile. Teams are supposed to provide pleasure and entertainment, not depression and disappointment.

It is also completely unnecessary to suffer several days' emotional devastation just because your team loses some big postseason deal like the Super Bowl. Why on earth would you place your happiness and peace of mind in the hands of several dozen strangers? Listen, folks, if they win, fine; if they lose, fuck 'em! Let 'em practice more. As for you, for Chrissakes find something to do! Get your ass down to the massage parlor and spring for a blow job.

If you really want to enjoy sports, do what I did. Become a Harlem Globetrotters fan. There's no losing, no stats, no strikes, no trades, no contract hassles, no postseason, and no annoying media. Just winning, all the time, every night. By the way, I'm just diseased enough to realize it would also be lots of fun to root for the Washington Generals, the team that loses to the Globetrotters every night. At least you wouldn't have to put up with all that annoying, preseason optimism bullshit.

One common American sports gripe I do not share: I am not like those radio call-in, sports-fan asswipes who think athletes are overpaid. I believe the players should get any amount of money they want, and the fans should go fuck themselves. I'm tired of fans whining all that weak shit about how "we pay their salaries" and "without us there would be no games." Bullshit! Fuck you! If you don't want to spend the money, stay the fuck home! And shut your mouth. Sports fans eat shit.

Sports fans rate even lower than the media and the franchise owners on my scale of miserable, shit-eating vermin. Here's the descending hierarchy: athletes, sports media, team owners, fans. Fans on the bottom. Most sports fans are fat, ignorant, beer-soaked, loudmouth, racist, white male cocksuckers, and they're totally unnecessary to the playing of the games.

The athletes are the only people in sports who count; they're the only one who are indispensable. Everyone else is superfluous. Think about it. The entire pro-sports sewer began because groups of men got together and played these games in parks, vacant lots, and gyms simply for the fun of it. No money involved; just personal bets. And if today, all the owners, media, and sports fans suddenly disappeared, the athletes would simply go back to the parks, vacant lots, and gyms and play the games by themselves. No one else is necessary.

Of course, if they did, the usual dull people who lack direction would stand around watching, and some businessman-asshole would get the idea of charging admission and giving the players a tiny percentage of the money, and the whole miserable pool of steaming liquid shit would start all over again.

But in spite of all these negative feelings, I still enjoy watching a good close game played by well-matched teams. Lots of scoring, a few good fights, and then preferably forty innings or an octuple overtime, so that both teams eventually run out of players, and many of them are injured because they're tired.

The score of the game is not the only thing I'm interested in. I also root very hard for slumps, losing streaks, penalties, fights, injuries, team dissension, athletes cracking under pressure, and widespread gambling scandals. An earthquake in a ballpark isn't such a bad thing to me, either. I don't give a shit about the outcome of the game, I'm just looking for an interesting story.

I pray that some year the baseball postseason will include only teams with outdoor stadiums in cold-weather cities. And then I hope there are repeated freak storm systems that keep coming through the Midwest and the East, and all during the playoffs there are constant rainouts and postponements. And I pray for the whole thing to continue for months, so the games are pushed further and further back, and eventually the World Series is played in January. And then I hope it's cold and windy and icy and snowy, and a lot of players get hurt, and the games turn out to be a national disgrace. That's the kind of shit I root for.

Then there are other times when I'm not as positive. And I think to myself, Fuck sports! Fuck sweat, fuck jock itch, and fuck all people who are out of breath. Fuck the players, the sports media, the owners, and above all, the sports fans. Double-fuck the sports fans. Actually, though, to tell you the truth, if I had to endure those owners on the same day-to-day basis as I do the sports fans, I'm sure the owners would quickly work their way to the bottom of my list. Lower than a snake's ballbag. Remember, owners are always rotten people no matter what they own, and no matter where they turn up in life.

In their hatred for the players, the fans often forget that the real insects are the owners; the greedy swine owners who are always pleading poverty. In 1980, Nelson Doubleday paid $21.6 million for the Mets franchise. Today it's worth over $200 million. Where's the risk? And if it's so hard to make money in baseball, why are all these maggot entrepreneur-hustlers around the country so eager to pay $95 million for a last-place expansion team?

I'm not too thrilled with the sports media people, either. The talent is marginal, they bring nothing to the mix, and their palpable envy of the players is actually embarrassing. Many of these media stiffs were failed high school and college athletes and simply not good enough to make the cut. (Obviously, I'm excluding former pro ballplayers.) How dare such also-rans criticize athletes and their play? You wanna know the problem? Athletes get tons of money and pussy, and all the best drugs. The sports media don't. Need any more on that?

Some baseball teams hire "ball girls" to retrieve foul balls that don't go into the stands. But I've noticed many of these women are quite feminine and don't throw very well. These teams are making a mistake. I think they should hire lesbians to do that job. Not femmes, but full-on, bad-ass, 90-mile-an hour bull dykes. The kind you see in hardware stores. I'll tell you one thing, you'd get a lot more good plays and strong return throws out there. And if some fan leaned out of the stands to pick up a foul ball, the "ball dyke" could drag him onto the field and beat the shit out of him for about forty-five minutes. And if any baseball players tried to stop her, she could just deck them, too.

Athletes like that physical shit. When they're pleased with each other they bump chests, butt heads, and bang forearms. Why don't they just punch each other in the fuckin' teeth? Wouldn't that be great? Teammates, I mean. After a touch-down pass, why doesn't the guy who caught the ball just go over and kick the quarterback right in the nuts? Same with a slam dunk in basketball. The guy who scores oughta grab a chair and beat the living shit out of the guy who fed him the ball. For about forty-five minutes. If this type of celebration were more common, the postgame show from the winners' locker room would be a lot livelier.

And I think there should be at least one sport where the object is to kill someone. A team sport. Deathball. Let's face it, athletes are mostly physical freaks with serious personality defects where competition is concerned, and they just love someone to "motivate" them. Well, what greater motivation can there be than trying to avoid being killed? It's a fuckin' natural! And for me, what could be more fun than watching one of these jackoffs motivate his ugly ass into an early grave every game?

Here's another thing: I love losing streaks. I wish some year a baseball team would lose 162 games. I especially like decades-long, postseason losing streaks. In fact, as soon as my teams are out of the running, I start actively rooting for the Cubs, Red Sox, Bills, Broncos, and Vikings to get as far as they can in the postseason so that ultimately they can let the big prize slip away one more time. I think it is an infinitely more interesting news story for a team to repeatedly fail at the high-est level than it is for them to finally win. If the Cubs ever win a World Series, the news coverage will be the most boring bunch of shit you can imagine.

And, although I wouldn't wish it on anyone, you'll have to admit it would sure be a lot of fun to see a couple of those chartered planes the athletes fly around in go down in flames. I know it might seem ghoulish to the overly squeamish, but I'd love to read about all the hassles they were having restocking the teams, and it would be fun to see the new lineups. Of course, all the stupid shit on TV about the funerals would be real boring.

P.S. Any professional sports team that has a "fight song" is automatically a bush-league, small-town team. Period.

FUCK YOU, I LIKE THESE KINDS OF JOKES!

Anticlimax: What my uncle was good at.

Chess: The piece movement.

Seersucker: A person who blows clairvoyants.

Passing gear: Clothing worn by light-skinned blacks who wish to be thought of as white.

Outspoken: When you lose a debate.

Hormone: The sound a prostitute makes so you'll think you're a real good fuck.

Drug traffic: Driving to your connection's house.

Sex drive: Similar to drug traffic, but with a different destination.

Douche: A female duke.

Octopus: An eight-sided vagina.

Trampoline: A sexual lubricant popular with sluts.

Parakeet: A keet that takes care of you until the real keet arrives.

Pussyfoot: A rare female birth defect requiring the use of open-toed shoes.

Beer nuts: The official disease of Milwaukee.

Cotton balls: The final stage of beer nuts.

Cowhand: An occupational disability common among dairy farmers.

Woodpecker: A seventeenth-century prosthetic device.

Leatherette: A short sadomasochist.

Cap pistol: A small gun that can be hidden in your hat.

A gay barbarian: Attila the hon.

"LET'S BEAT THEM WITH OUR PURSES!"

The reason for most violence against gays is that heterosexual men are forced to prove that they, themselves, are not gay. It goes like this: Men in strong male subcultures like the police, the military, and sports (and a few other cesspools) bond very strongly. Hunting, fishing, and golfing friendships also produce this unnatural bonding. These guys bond and bond, and get closer and closer, until finally they're just drunk enough to say, "You know, I really love these guys." And that frightens them. So they must quickly add, "But I'm not a queer!"

See the dilemma? Now they have to go out of their way to prove to the world, to their buddies, and to themselves that they don't harbor homoerotic feelings. And it's only a short step from "I"m not a queer" to "In fact, I hate queers!" And another short step to "Let's go kill some queers!" And what they really seek to kill is not the queer outside, it's the queer inside they fear.

Gay bashers are repressed homosexuals attempting to deny the queer inside, but certain signals get past the screen. That's why you see so many policemen with those precious little well-groomed mustaches. You'd see more of those same mustaches on athletes and military men, but those two groups are not allowed to express themselves freely. Military drones and many sheep-like athletes have dress codes and are forbidden to wear facial hair. The idea is to limit and reduce their individuality. These are men who have chosen to allow "the organization" to run their lives. That's why athletes, police, and military men have that rigid unbending body language; they're severely repressed. Guess what they're repressing? And, hey, why do you think they call those police cars "cruisers"?

SIGNS

I have a suggestion that I think would help fight serious crime. Signs. There are lots of signs for minor infractions: No Smoking, Stay Off the Grass, Keep Out, and they seem to work fairly well. I think we should also have signs for major crimes: Murder Strictly Prohibited, No Raping People, Thank You for Not Kidnapping Anyone. It's certainly worth a try. I'm convinced Watergate would never have happened if there had just been a sign in the Oval Office that said, Malfeasance of Office Is Strictly Against the Law, or Thank You for Not Undermining the Constitution.

When you drive through an entrance or exit lane that has one of those signs, Do Not Back Up—Severe Tire Damage, and you're going in the correct direction, don't you sort of worry about it anyway? That maybe they got it wrong? Or somebody turned the sign around? Or some guy on drugs installed the spikes? Or maybe *you're* on drugs, and you think, Am I doing this right? Am I backing up? No, I seem to be going forward. Let's see. Which way are the spikes pointing? Oh, I can't see the spikes anymore. I guess I better back up a little.

Here's a sign I don't like: Authorized Personnel Only. Now, if there's one thing I know about myself, it's that I am definitely not authorized. I wouldn't even know where to go to *get* authorized. Can you do it by mail? Wouldn't baptism sort of authorize you? It doesn't matter; I go through the door anyway. If I get stopped, I say, "Well, I may not be authorized for this, but I am authorized for other things. And your sign doesn't mention which things."

I've got a terrific sign in front of my house that keeps intruders out: Retarded Pit Bull High on Angel Dust. No one's come over the wall yet. Except a couple of retarded guys who were high on angel dust.

DO, TAKE, HAVE, GIVE

People used to *take* drugs, now they *do* drugs. Some people don't do *drugs*, they do *lunch*. Instead of taking *drugs*, they take *meetings*. They used to *have* meetings. Now, instead of having *meetings*, they have *relationships*. Some people who don't do drugs but have a relationship will take a meeting while they do lunch.

People used to *get* sex, now they *have* sex. So far, they don't *do* sex. Although they do say, "Let's do it." But if the sex is overly aggressive, we say the person was "taken." I guess if one's not giving, the other's gonna take.

We take a lot of things. We take a lot of *good* things. We take time, we take heart, we take solace, medicine, advice; we take a job, take a break, take a vacation, a leave, a nap, a rest, a seat, we take a meal.

We take, take, take until we can't take anymore. Maybe it's because our inner nature is not primarily one of giving, but of taking. Even these things we take that should balance our lives and give us rest do not. We make work out of them. We do them aggressively; always in control. Take.

But when we give, we give a lot of bad things. We give trouble, heartache, sorrow, we give someone a hard time, a migraine, give 'em a heart attack, and give 'em a big pain in the ass.

So I say, "Give up, get fucked, take a hike, and have fun."

YOU'RE A NATURAL

This is for health food fiends, the natural-fabrics gang, and all those green-head environmental hustlers who stomp around in the "natural": Your key word is meaningless. Everything is natural. Everything in the universe is a part of nature. Polyester, pesticides, oil slicks, and whoopee cushions. Nature is not just trees and flowers. It's everything. Human beings are part of nature. And if a human being invents something, that's part of nature, too. Like the whoopee cushion.

Also: The experience called "natural childbirth" is not natural at all. It is freaky and bizarre. It is distinctly unnatural for a person to invite and welcome pain. Whose influence am I sensing here? Men's? It's nothing more than childbirth machisma. The woman wants it said of her that she can "take it like a man."

GOOD FOR HEADACHES

Sometimes on television they tell you a product is "good for headaches." I don't want something that's good for headaches. I want something that's bad for headaches. And good for me.

THROW YOUR BACK OUT

Several months ago, a friend told me that when he was cleaning his garage he threw his back out. I told him it was probably overenthusiasm. Sometimes when you're cleaning, you get carried away and throw out something you intended to keep. The next time I ran into him he seemed to have learned his lesson. He had recently cleaned out his attic, but this time he didn't throw his back out. He gave it to Goodwill.

FIRST THINGS FIRST

Many things we take for granted must have sounded unusual the first time they were proposed. For instance, imagine trying to explain to someone, for the first time, that you thought giving him an enema would be a real good idea. You'd have to proceed very subtly.

"Hey, Joey! I got a new idea. Turn around."

"New id–? Hey, what's that thing in your hand?"

"Nothing. Oh! I dropped my keys. Would you mind pickin' 'em up?"

Or imagine the very first guy who threw up. What did he think? What did he say to his friends? "Hey, Vinny, c'mere! Remember that yak we ate? Look!"

UNNECESSARY WORDS

There is a tendency these days to complicate speech by adding unnecessary words. The following phrases all contain at least one word too many.

emergency situation

shower activity

surgical procedure

boarding process

flotation device

hospital environment

fear factor

free of charge

knowledge base

forest setting

beverage items

prison setting

peace process

intensity level

belief system

seating area

sting operation

evacuation process

rehabilitation process

facial area

daily basis

blue in color

risk factor

crisis situation

leadership role

learning process

rain event

confidence level

healing process

standoff situation

shooting incident

planning process

The best known example of this problem is: "At that point in time." I've even heard people say, "At that particular point in time." Boy, that's pinning it down, isn't it?

This typing process is beginning to tire out my finger area. Not to mention what it's doing to my mind situation. I think it's time to consider the break factor here, before I have a fatigue incident.

SHORT TAKES (Part 1)

the wisest man I ever knew taught me something I never forgot. And although I never forgot it, I never quite memorized it either. So what I'm left with is the memory of having learned something very wise that I can't quite remember.

Just what exactly is the "old dipsy doodle"?

When I hear a person talking about political solutions, I know I am not listening to a serious person.

Sties are caused by watching your dog shit.

SOMETIMES A LITTLE BRAIN DAMAGE CAN HELP

A woman told me her child was autistic, and I thought she said artistic. So I said, "Oh, great. I'd like to see some of the things he's done."

Eventually there will come a time when everyone is in a band.

Weyerhauser, a company that makes its money by cutting down trees, calls itself "The tree-growing company."

If a man smiles all the time he's probably selling something that doesn't work.

Not only do I not know what's going on, I wouldn't know what to do about it if I did.

How likely is it that all the people who are described as missing are living together in a small town somewhere?

We're all fucked. It helps to remember that.

If lobsters looked like puppies, people could never drop them in boiling water while they're still alive. But instead, they look like science fiction monsters, so it's OK. Restaurants that allow patrons to select live lobsters from a tank should be made to paint names on their shells: "Happy," "Baby Doll," "Junior." I defy anyone to drop a living thing called "Happy" in rapidly boiling water.

The nicest thing about anything is not knowing what it is.

I feel sorry for homeless gay people; they have no closet to come out of. In fact, I imagine if you *were* gay and homeless, you'd probably be glad just to *have* a closet.

I've adopted a new lifestyle that doesn't require my presence. In fact, if I don't want to, I don't have to get out of bed at all, and I still get credit for a full day.

The sicker you get, the harder it is to remember if you took your medicine.

I can't bear to go to the children's zoo. I always wonder how their parents can allow them to be kept in those little cages.

If you take the corn off the cob, not only do you have corn-off-the-cob, you also have cobs-out-from-inside-the-corn.

Why do foreign soldiers march funny? Do they think we march funny? If we do, how would we know?

If you mail a letter to the post office, who delivers it?

O n the fritz" is a useful expression only if you're talking about a home appliance. You wouldn't say, "The Space Shuttle is on the fritz." You'd never hear it in a hospital. "Doctor, the heart-lung machine is on the fritz."

Rarely does a loose woman have a tight pussy.

Some see the glass as half-empty, some see the glass as half-full. I see the glass as too big.

My uncle thought he would clean up in dirt farming, but prices fell, and he took a real bath. Eventually, he washed his hands of the whole thing.

Kilometers are shorter than miles. Save gas, take your next trip in kilometers.

Test of metal: Will of iron, nerves of steel, heart of gold, balls of brass.

WHITE PEOPLE FUCKED UP THE BLUES

If you love someone, set them free; if they come home, set them on fire.

I've never owned a telescope, but it's something I'm thinking of looking into.

Whenever I see a large crowd, I always wonder what was the most disgusting thing any one of them ever did.

I think they ought to let guys like Jeffrey Dahmer off with a warning. They do it with speeding tickets. Sometimes all a guy needs is a good talking to. Why don't they say, "Listen, Jeff. Knock it off! Nobody thinks you're funny. Eat one more guy and we're comin' after ya."

hey kids! It's mostly bullshit and garbage, and none of the stuff they tell you is true. And when your dumb-ass father says he wants you to amount to something, he means make a lot of money. How do you think the word *amount* got in there?

Those nicotine patches seem to work pretty well, but I understand it's kind of hard to keep 'em lit.

in El Salvador, they declared a cease fire after ten years. Why didn't they think of that at the beginning? Anyway, the best thing about El Salvador is that they killed a lot of religious people. How often do you get 10 percent of the body count in clergy?

At one point in my haste to improve myself, I mixed up the telephone numbers of the Shick Center for the Control of Smoking and the Evelyn Woods Speed Reading School. As a result, I can now smoke up to 300 cigarettes a minute, but I gave up reading.

Preschool teacher": If it's not a school, why do they need a teacher? Don't they need a "preteacher"?

Most people are not particularly good at anything.

how can someone be "armed with a handgun"? Shouldn't he be armed with an "armgun"? Can a handgun really be a sidearm? And shouldn't a hand grenade be an arm grenade? You don't throw it with your hand, you throw it with your arm.

Try explaining Hitler to a kid.

FUCK AL JOLSON

Why do we turn lights "out" when we turn most other things "off"?

The straightest line between a short distance is two points.

Working-class people "look for work." Middle-class people "try to get a job." Upper-middle-class people "seek employment."

Can you have just one antic? How about a lone shenanigan? A monkeyshine?

There are two pips in a beaut, four beauts in a lulu, eight lulus in a doozy, and sixteen doozies in a humdinger. No one knows how many humdingers there are in a lollapalooza.

It is a sad thing to see an Indian wearing a cowboy hat.

Those who dance are considered insane by those who can't hear the music.

THERE WILL BE NO MORE PAPER TOWELS AFTER JULY

It is impossible to know accurately how you look in your sunglasses.

As he ages, Mickey Rooney gets even shorter.

Elevators and escalators do more than elevate and escalate. They also lower. The names tell only half the story.

No one ever refers to "half a month."

Don't you get discouraged each morning when you wake up and realize you have to wash again?

You show me the people who control the money, the land, and the weapons, and I'll show you the people in charge.

I'm not going to apologize for this, but I have my own personal psychic. He doesn't predict the future, and he can't tell you much about your past. But he does a really fantastic job of describing the present. For instance, he can tell you exactly what you're wearing, but he can't do it over the phone.

We're all amateurs; it's just that some of us are more professional about it than others.

When the going gets tough, the tough get fucked.

I was expelled from cooking school, and it left a bad taste in my mouth.

ast year, in Los Angeles, a robber threatened a store owner with a syringe that he claimed had HIV on it, saying "Give me the money or I'll give you AIDS." You know what I would've told him? "If you give me AIDS I'm gonna find your wife and daughter and fuck them."

I think we should attack Russia now. They'd never expect it.

I have as much authority as the Pope, I just don't have as many people who believe it.

What is the plural of "a hell of a guy"? "Hells of guys"?

The phrase *surgical strike* might be more acceptable if it were common practice to perform surgery with high explosives.

I never eat sushi. I have trouble eating things that are merely unconscious.

When you find existing time on a parking meter, you should be able to add it to the end of your life. Minus the time you spent on hold.

I recently went to a new doctor and noticed he was located in something called the Professional Building. I felt better right away.

You can't fight City Hall, but you can goddamn sure blow it up.

Just think, right now as you read this, some guy somewhere is gettin' ready to hang himself.

JESUS WAS A CROSS-DRESSER

I have no ax to grind, but I do have an ivory letter opener that could use sharpening.

feminists want to ban pornography on the grounds that it encourages violence against women. The Japanese consume far more violent and depraved pornography than we do, and yet there is almost no rape reported there. A woman is twenty times more in danger of being raped in the U.S. than she is in Japan. Why? Because Japanese people are decent, civilized, and intelligent.

The only good thing ever to come out of religion was the music.

I don't have to tell you it goes without saying there are some things better left unsaid. I think that speaks for itself. The less said about it the better.

Do kings have sweat bands in their crowns?

When someone is impatient and says, "I haven't got all day," I always wonder, How can that be? How can you not have all day?

There ought to be at least one round state.

for a long time it was all right for a woman to keep a diary, but it sounded too fruity for men. So they changed it to *journal*. Now sensitive men can set down their thoughts without appearing *too* sensitive.

In comic strips the person on the left always speaks first.

A courtesy bus driver once told me to go fuck myself.

Sometimes the label on the can says "fancy peas." Then, you get 'em home and they're really rather ordinary. Nothing fancy about 'em , at all. Maybe if they had little bullfight paintings on them, they would be fancy. But as it is . . .

SLAP A DEAD PERSON

If the shoe fits, get another one just like it.

Eventually, nature will produce a species that can play the piano better than we can.

I don't think we really gave barbarism a fair try.

Piano lessons sound like something a piano should take. Humans should take piano-playing lessons.

Did you hear about the man who left in a huff and returned in a jiffy? Another day, he arrived in a tizzy and left in a snit. His wife swept in in a fury and left in a daze, then left in a dither and returned in a whirl.

If you go to a bone bank, why can't you make a calcium deposit?

"Get down!" is a slang expression that would have been really useful in World War II. If soldiers had known this expression at the time, a lot of lives could have been saved.

WHY CAN'T THERE BE MORE SUFFERING?

There are no times that don't have moments like these.

Since 1983, more than thirty people have been killed in post office shootings. You know why? Because the price of stamps keeps changing. There's a lot of pressure. "How much are they now, Rob? Twenty-nine? Thirty-two? I can't keep track! Fuck it!" BANG BANG BANG BANG BANG BANG BANG BANG BANG!!!

On Opening Day, the President doesn't throw *out* the first ball. He throws it *in*. If he threw it out, it would land in the parking lot and someone would have to go get it.

Where does the dentist go when he leaves you alone?

Why are there never any really good-looking women on long distance buses?

I almost don't feel the way I do.

We're not satisfied with forcing Russia to destroy its nuclear weapons and recant its ideology. Now we're really going to get even: we're sending experts to show them how to run their economy. Am I missing something? A country with a five-trillion-dollar debt is giving advice on handling money?

She "took him to the cleaners." Whenever I hear that I wonder if that was the only errand he had to run. Maybe she also took him to the adult bookstore.

I go to bed early. My favorite dream comes on at nine.

best seller" really only means "good seller." There can only be one best seller. All the rest are good sellers. Each succeeding book on the list is a "better seller."

There should be some things we don't name, just so we can sit around all day and wonder what they are.

Everything is still the same. It's just a little different now.

The symphony orchestra had played poorly, so the conductor was in a bad mood. That night he beat his wife—because the music hadn't been beautiful enough.

You know why I stopped eating processed foods? I began to picture the people who might be processing them.

Whenever I see a large crowd I always think of all the dry cleaning they have out.

I didn't wash today. I wasn't dirty. If I'm not dirty, I don't wash. Some weeks I don't have to shower at all. I just groom my three basic areas: teeth, hair, and asshole. And to save time, I use the same brush.

I AM NOT IN COMPLIANCE

When you buy a six-foot dildo, and call it a marital aid, you are stretching not just the anatomy, but the limits of credibility.

At a formal dinner party, the person nearest death should always be seated closest to the bathroom.

The child molester skipped breakfast, but said he'd grab a little something on the way to work.

tHINGS YOU DON'T WANT TO HEAR: "Jeff? We're going to have to break your skull again and reset it. Okay? It's way out of line. It looks really strange. But we won't do it until we've opened up that incision and put some more fire ants inside of you. OK?"

In Panama, during the election that defeated Noriega, there were "dignity battalions" that wandered the streets beating and robbing and killing people.

Someone said to me, "Make yourself a sandwich." Well, if I could make myself a sandwich, I wouldn't make myself a sandwich. I'd make myself a horny, 18-year-old billionaire.

Why would anyone want to use a flood light? I should think lights would be kind of dangerous during a flood. Better just to sit in the dark and wait for help.

There are nights when the wolves are silent, and only the moon howls.

The nicest thing about a plane crashing at an air show is that they always have good video of the actual crash.

How come none of these boxers seem to have a losing record?

Where ideas are concerned, America can be counted on to do one of two things: take a good idea and run it completely into the ground, or take a bad idea and run it completely into the ground.

If I only had one tooth, I think I would brush it a real long time.

If we could just find out who's in charge, we could kill him.

Whenever I hear that someone works in his shirtsleeves, I always wonder what he did with the rest of the shirt.

It is impossible to dry one hand.

The word *bipartisan* usually means some larger-than-usual deception is being carried out.

I saw an old woman who I thought was looking on the ground for a contact lens. As I drew closer, I realized she was actually all hunched over from osteoporosis.

GERMS LIVE IN MY HAT

You can lead a gift horse to water in the middle of the stream, but you can't look him in the mouth and make him drink.

deep Throat: Think about it. There is actually an important figure in American history who is named for a blow-job movie. How do grade-school teachers handle this?

Regarding the fitness craze: America has lost its soul; now it's trying to save its body.

Nothing is so boring as listening to someone else describe a dream.

hat is all this stuff about a kick being "partially blocked"? It's either blocked, not blocked, or deflected. Partially blocked is like "somewhat dead."

I notice I don't see as many buck-toothed women as I used to.

The thing I like the most about this country is that, in a pinch, when things really get tough, you can always go into a store and buy some mints.

I've watched so many documentaries about World War II, I'm sure I've seen the same people die hundreds of times.

I'll bet there aren't too many people hooked on crack who can play the bag-pipes.

I read that some guy was giving up the governor's chair to run for a Senate seat. Why would he give up a chair to run for a seat? Why not be a judge and sit on the bench?

How do primitive people know if they're doing the dances correctly?

THINGS YOU NEVER HEAR: "Please stop sucking my dick or I'll call the police."

Regarding smoking in public: Suppose you were eating in a restaurant, and every two minutes the guy at the next table threw some anthrax germs in the air. Wouldn't you want to sit in a different section?

The savings-and-loan associations that will cost $500 billion to bail out are called "the thrifts."

The idea of a walk-in closet sounds frightening. If I'm ever sittin' at home and a closet walks in, I'm gettin' outta there.

The reason they call it the American Dream is because you have to be asleep to believe it.

I'D RATHER
BE COMING

How can there possibly be a self-addressed envelope? They say now they even have envelopes that are self-sealing. This I gotta see!

I saw a sign: Park and ride. It's confusing. They really oughta make up their minds.

Park and lock. Here we go again. If you park and lock, you're stuck in the car. It should be park, get out, and lock.

"No comment" is a comment.

Why is it like this? Why isn't everything different?

If you have chicken at lunch and chicken at dinner, do you ever wonder if the two chickens knew each other?

She was only a prostitute, but she had the nicest face I ever came across.

It's odd that the word *breath* becomes *breathe* by adding a letter at the end, and yet the pronunciation changes in the middle. And *woman* becomes *women* by changing the vowel at the end, while the pronunciation changes near the beginning. Was somebody drunk when these decisions were made?

Russia actually has something called *vodka riots*.

I think it would be fun to go on "Jeopardy" and never buzz in. Just stand there for half an hour, never talk, and then go home.

Diplomatic immunity is necessary, because of the many diseases diplomats are exposed to in foreign countries.

Why is San Francisco in the "bay area," but Saudi Arabia is in the "gulf region"? Is a region really bigger than an area?

Whenever I hear about a spy ring, I always wonder if that's the only jewelry they wear. You'd think a spy wouldn't want to call attention to himself with a lot of flashy jewelry. For instance, you never hear about a spy necklace.

THIS IS JUST SOME PRINTING

It's better if an entire family gets Alzheimer's disease. That way they can all sit around and wonder who they are.

Time sharing got a bad name, so now they call it "interval ownership."

Harness racing may be all right for some people, but I prefer watching the horses.

If you get cheated by the Better Business Bureau, who do you complain to?

As soon as a person tells you they have a surprise for you, they have lost the element of surprise.

I saw a picture of the inventor of the hydrogen bomb, Edwin Teller, wearing a tie clip. Why would the man who invented a bomb that destroys everything for fifty miles be concerned about whether or not his tie was straight?

No one calls you "Bub" anymore.

Why is there such controversy about drug testing? I know plenty of guys who'd be willing to test any drug they can come up with.

If the Cincinnati Reds were really the first major league baseball team, who did they play?

I AM REPELLED BY WHOLESOMENESS

When they say someone is making a "personal tour," are they suggesting that, on the other hand, it is somehow possible to make a tour without actually being there?

After how much time does a persistent cough become a chronic cough?

Intelligence tests are biased toward the literate.

The carousel and Ferris wheel owners traveled in different circles so they rarely made the rounds together.

Which is more immoral? Killing two 100-pound people or killing one 300-pound person?

guest host is a bad enough oxymoron, but NBC raised the stakes when, a few years back, they installed Jay Leno as the "permanent guest host." Not to be outdone, Joan Rivers pointed out that she had been the "first permanent guest host." Check, please!

I don't own a camera, so I travel with a police sketch artist.

if JFK Jr. got into a taxi in New York to go to the airport, do you think he would say, "Take me to JFK?" How would he feel about that? And how does Lee Harvey Oswald's mother feel when she walks through JFK, knowing that if she had stayed single it would probably be Martin Luther King Jr. Airport?

Which is taller, a short-order cook or a small-engine mechanic?

Hobbies are for people who lack direction.

FUCK SOCCER MOMS

A graveyard always has to start with a single body. Unless the local people get lucky and there's a nice big bus accident in town.

A lot of times when they catch a guy who killed twenty-seven people, they say, "He was a loner." Well, of course he was a loner; he killed everyone he came in contact with.

Is it illegal to charge admission to a free-for-all?

read about some mob guy who was being charged with gambling, loan sharking, extortion, narcotics, prostitution, murder, pornography, labor racketeering, stolen cars, business fraud, mail fraud, wire fraud, bribery, corruption, perjury, and jury tampering. Here's a guy who didn't waste a minute. Busy, busy, busy!

My definition of bad luck: catching AIDS from a Quaker.

Dogs and cats get put to sleep, hogs and cows get slaughtered.

If a speed freak went to Rapid City to make a quick buck in fast food he might sell instant coffee in an express lane.

I worry about my judgment when anything I believe in or do regularly begins to be accepted by the American public.

Imagine how thick Japanese people's photo albums must be.

Some national parks have long waiting lists for camping reservations. I think when you have to wait a year to sleep next to a tree, something is wrong.

When football fans tear down the goalpost, where do they take it?

Just because your penis surgery was not successful is no reason to go off half-cocked.

In England in 1830, William Hukkison became the first person ever run over by a railroad train. Wouldn't that make you feel stupid? For millions and millions of years there were no trains, and then suddenly they have trains and you get run over?

NOTHING RHYMES WITH NOSTRIL

Shouldn't a complimentary beverage tell you what a fine person you are?

Only Americans could find as a prime means of self-expression the wave and the high five.

It is important to remember that although the Automobile Club has a health plan, the health club does not have an automobile plan.

Auto racing: slow minds and fast cars.

If you fuck a baseball player's wife while he's on the road, his team will lose the next day.

If Helen Keller had psychic ability, would you say she had a fourth sense?

Why do the Dutch people have two names for their country, Holland and the Netherlands, and neither one includes the word *Dutch*?

Late one night it struck me that for several years I had been masturbating to a Wilma Flintstone fantasy.

Why do we say *redheaded* but *brownhaired*?

does the water that signifies the passage of time flow under the bridge, or over the dam? I've heard both versions, and I'm concerned about the people who live near the dam.

In the movies, when someone buys something they never wait for their change.

I buy stamps by mail. It works OK until I run out of stamps.

Whenever someone tells me they're going to fix a chicken, I always think, Maybe it isn't really broken. Maybe it just needs a little oil.

My only superstition: if you drop a spoon, a wild pig will offer to finance your next car.

As a matter of principle I never attend the first annual anything.

Why is it with any piece of home electronics equipment there are always a few buttons and switches you never use?

There is actually a show on the lifetime channel called "Dentistry Update."

When you eat two different types of candy bars in succession, the second one is not as easy to enjoy because you get so used to how good the first one tastes.

BLOOD IS THICKER
THAN URINE

They said some guy arrested for murder in Las Vegas had "a history of questionable actions." Can you imagine if we were all held to that standard?

There is no will, and there is no wisdom.

Some people like to watch "monster trucks" drive on top of cars and crush them. Then there are the other people who can't get to the arena, because they don't have cars.

A lot of these people who keep a gun at home for safety are the same ones who refuse to wear a seat belt.

It's legal for men to be floorwalkers and illegal for women to be streetwalkers.

Look at the self-help titles in the bookstore, and you'll get a fews clues about our culture. They're all about aggression and acquisition. It wouldn't be at all surprising to see a book called *How to Force Your Will on Other People by Giving Them the Shaft and Fucking Them out of Their Money*.

When you sneeze, all the numbers in your head go up by one.

How can *crash course* and *collision course* have two different meanings?

I wanted to get a job as a gynecologist, but I couldn't find an opening.

Why don't they have dessert at breakfast?

Sometimes I look out the airplane window at a large city at night and wonder how many people are fucking.

Why don't they have rye pancakes? Grapefruit cookies? Fig ice cream? Canteloupe pie?

The *mai tai* got its name when two Polynesian alcoholics got in a fight over some neckwear.

I hope they do clone the dinosaurs, and they come back just in time for the ozone layer to disappear and wipe those ugly motherfuckers out again.

In most polls there are always about 5 percent of the people who "don't know." What isn't generally understood is that it's the same people in every poll.

I read that a patient got AIDS from his dentist. It wasn't from the blood; apparently, the dentist fucked him in the ass. "Open wide!"

Regarding Red Riding Hood: Wolves can't be all bad if they'll eat your grandmother. Even Grandpa won't do that.

I think we've outgrown the word *gripe*. When everyone has automatic weapons, a word like *gripe* is sort of irrelevant.

PIG SNERV

"The friendly skies." "The skies are not cloudy." How is this possible? I look up, I see one sky.

Kids are now being born with syphilis *and* cocaine habits. There's nothing like waking up your second day on Earth and realizing that once you kick cocaine you're still gonna have the syph. And hey, kids! If you didn't get VD in the womb, don't worry, you still have a shot. Some toddlers recently picked up gonorrhea at a day care center.

I always thought a semi-truck driver was someone who dropped out of truck-driving school halfway through the course.

When Sammy Davis Jr. kissed a woman, do you think he closed his bad eye?

Environmentalists changed the word *jungle* to *rain forest*, because no one would give them money to save a jungle. Same with *swamps* and *wetlands*.

When a lion escapes from a circus in Africa, how do they know when they've caught the right one?

The safest place to be during an earthquake would be in a stationary store.

Wouldn't it be funny if you went to group therapy and the Mills Brothers were there?

I'm not an organ donor, but I once gave an old piano to the Salvation Army.

Cancer research is a growth industry.

Sometimes I sit for hours weighing the fine distinctions among *spunk*, *pluck*, *balls*, *nerve*, *chutzpah*, *gall*, and *moxie*.

It is impossible for an abortion clinic to have a waiting list of more than nine months.

YOU NEVER SEE A SMILING RUNNER

Carjackings, smash-and-grabs, snipers, home invasions, follow-home robberies, hostage incidents, barricade/standoff situations, drive-by shootings, walk-up shootings, traffic shootings, pipe bombs, mail bombs. Shit! We never had cool crimes like that when I was a kid. All we had was robbery and murder. I feel deprived.

In a hotel, why can't you use the house phone to phone your house?

I'm bringing out my own line of colognes. You've heard of Eternity, Obsession, and Passion? Mine is Stench! I'm offering a choice of five fragrances: Bait Shop, Animal Waste, Landfill, Human Remains, and Chemical Toilet.

When I was a kid I used to think it was all the same clouds that kept coming by.

SOMETHING IS DREADFULLY WRONG IN THIS COUNTRY: There is now an "empathy breast." It is a wrap-around vest that has a pocket for placing the baby's bottle in. The new father wears it while "nursing" the baby. Jesus!

Sometimes on a rainy day I sit around and weed the losers out of my address book.

they said on the news that tests on monkeys showed HIV can be transmitted through oral sex. What I want to know is, who had to blow the monkeys?

The other night I ate at a real nice family restaurant. Every table had an argument going.

I don't live in the fast lane, but have you ever seen one of those cars parked on the median with its hood up?

just think, right now, all over the world there are people exercising bad judgment. Somebody, right this minute, is probably making the mistake of his life.

Poor confetti. Its useful life lasts about two seconds. And it can never be used again.

human beings are kind of interesting from birth until they reach the age of a year and a half. Then they are boring until they reach fifty. By that time they're either completely defeated and fucked up, which makes them interesting again, or they've learned how to beat the game, and that makes them interesting, too.

THINK OFF-CENTER

The older I get, the more certain I am that I will not have to spend the rest of my life in prison.

Assisted suicide is controversial. There are moral, medical, legal, and ethical arguments. But the truth of it is, a lot of people just want to get the fuck outta here.

What exactly do you do when the Dalai Lama appears on "Nightline," and you're not satisfied with his answers?

Whenever I see a picture of a group of people in the newspaper, I always wonder how many of them have had really depraved sex since the picture was taken.

A small town is any place too poor to have its own insane asylum.

exas canceled plans to put its motto, Friendship, on its license plates. People complained that it was too wimpy. Why don't they just change their motto? Let's Kill All the Niggers comes to mind as appropriate.

In Vienna, they recently had an opera riot.

Never get on an airplane if the pilot is wearing a hat that has more than three pastel colors.

Why is it when you buy five shirts, there's always one you never wear? To minimize this problem, when I shop for shirts I always put one back just before I pay.

My family and I are doing our bit for the environment. We've volunteered to have sixty metric tons of human waste stored in our home.

CANCER CAUSES HEART DISEASE

Shopping and buying and getting and having comprise the Great American Addiction. No one is immune: When the underclass riots in this country, they don't kill policemen and politicians, they steal merchandise. How embarrassing.

I made a bargain with the devil: I would get to be famous, and he would get to fuck my sister.

Granola bars didn't sell very well when they were good for you. Now they have caramel, chocolate, marshmallow, saturated fat, and sweeteners; and a small amount of oats and wheat. Sales picked up.

you know you're in trouble when you look behind the clerk and see one of your personal checks displayed on the wall as an example of why the store does not accept personal checks.

As grown-ups, we never get to "wave bye-bye." I think it would be fun. "Steve, the boss is sailing for Europe; we're all going down to the dock to wave bye-bye."

Some things a king never has to say:
"Can I play, too?"
"Hey, guys, wait for me."
"I never seem to get laid."

did you ever go somewhere and realize it used to be a different place? And it dawns on you that some things are not here anymore. Of course, some other things are not here *yet*. And nothing seems to be where it used to be; everything's been moved. Sometimes I think if we could just put everything back where it originally was, we might be all right.

I was surprised when I started getting old. I always thought it was one of those things that would happen to someone else.

ALUMINUM IS A JIVE METAL

You know you're in a poor neighborhood when you give the store clerk a dollar and he asks you if you have anything smaller.

Since childhood is a time when kids prepare to be grown-ups, I think it makes a lot of sense to completely traumatize your children. Gets 'em ready for the real world.

With all that humping going on, JFK's administration shouldn't have been called Camelot, they should have called it Come-a-lot.

There is a new British rock band called So Long, Mate! During each performance one member of the band is ritually slaughtered. The music has a certain urgency, but the tours are nice and short. About five days.

When the convention of testicle transplant surgeons had its annual softball game, they asked me to throw out the first ball.

You know what would be fun? Drop acid, smoke PCP, and then take the White House tour with Jim Carrey.

I don't believe there's any problem in this country, no matter how tough it is, that Americans, when they roll up their sleeves, can't completely ignore.

Sometimes a fireman will go to great, strenuous lengths to save a raccoon that's stuck in a drainpipe and then go out on the weekend and kill several of them for amusement.

They debated the NAFTA trade bill for a long time; should we sign it or not? Either way, the people get fucked. Trade always exists for the traders. Anytime you hear businessmen debating "which policy is better for America," don't bend over.

Property is theft. Nobody owns anything. When you die, it stays here. I read about these billionaires: Sam Walton 20 billion, Daniel Ludwig 15 billion. They're both dead. They're gone, and the money is still here. It wasn't their money to begin with. Property is theft.

If you want to keep your dog in line, walk him past the fur shop a couple of times a week.

There are only two places in the world: over here and over there.

MILK CHOCOLATE IS FOR SCHMUCKS

I have a photograph of Judge Bork, but it doesn't do him justice.

Have you ever wondered why Republicans are so interested in encouraging people to volunteer in their communities? It's because volunteers work for no pay. Republicans have been trying to get people to work for no pay for a long time.

I finally accepted Jesus. Not as my personal savior, but as a man I intend to borrow money from.

It used to be, cars had cool names: Dart, Hawk, Fury, Cougar, Firebird, Hornet, Mustang, Barracuda. Rocket 88! Now we have Elantra, Altima, Acura, Lumina, Sentra, Corolla, Maxima. Tercel! What the fuck kind of lifeless, pussy names are these? Further proof America has lost its edge.

I'm starting a campaign to have Finland removed as a country. We don't need it.

What a spot! You're in surgery, the anesthetic wears off, and as you wake up you realize that someone in surgical clothing is carrying one of your legs over to a garbage can. The surgeon, holding a large power saw, says, "We're all out of anesthetic, but if you'll hold on real tight to the sides of that gurney, I'll have that other leg off in a jiffy."

You rarely meet a wino with perfect pitch.

Although the photographer and the art thief were close friends, neither had ever taken the other's picture.

Traditional American values: Genocide, aggression, conformity, emotional repression, hypocrisy, and the worship of comfort and consumer goods.

I read that Domino's Pizza trucks have killed more than twenty people. And that's not counting the ones who eat the pizza.

I like it when a flower or a little tuft of grass grows through a crack in the concrete. It's so fuckin' heroic.

A group of cult people has emerged who not only believe Elvis Presley is alive, but have decided that if they find him they will kill and skin him.

there are ten thousand people in the United States in a persistent vegetative state. Just enough to start a small town. Think of them as veggie-burghers.

Apparently, the Hells Angels are suing a movie producer because they said his film shows disrespect for the Hells Angels. OK.

SIMON SAYS, GO FUCK YOURSELF

SOMETHING IS DREADFULLY WRONG IN THIS COUNTRY: There is actually an organization called Wrestlers Against Drugs, and on TV there is now a Christian weight-lifting tour.

I once read that in Lebanon a peacekeeping force was attacked by a religious militia. They deserve each other.

Ross Perot. Just what a nation of idiots needs: a short, loud idiot.

When you visualize the recent past, do you see it as being somewhere over on the left?

Now the brainless New Age spiritual zombies are using bulldozers to vandalize the Ouachita National Forest in Arkansas in search of crystals. Nothing like that being-in-harmony-with-nature shit.

In some places, a seventeen-year-old girl needs a note for being absent from school, but she does not need one to get an abortion.

There's a moment coming. It's not here yet. It's still on the way. It's in the future. It hasn't arrived. Here it comes. Here it is . . . shit! It's gone.

A sure way to cure hiccups is to jam your fist down the affected person's throat and quickly open and close your hand several times. It relaxes the vega nerve.

SOMETHING IS DREADFULLY WRONG IN THIS COUNTRY: In a November 1990 Gallup Poll of 1,108 Americans, 78 percent said they believed there was a place where people who had led good lives were eternally rewarded, and 60 percent believed there was a place where those who led bad lives and died without repentance were eternally damned. I find this profoundly disturbing.

I always order the International Breakfast: French toast, English muffin, Belgian waffle, Spanish omelet, Danish pastry, Swedish pancakes, Canadian bacon, and Irish Coffee.

THERE ARE GHOSTS IN MY SINUSES

regarding local residents attempting to ban sex shops from their neighborhoods: You show me a parent who says he's worried about his child's innocence, and I'll show you a homeowner trying to maintain equity.

I thought it would be nice to get a job at a duty-free shop, but it doesn't sound like there's a whole lot to do in a place like that.

there's an odd feeling you get when someone on the sidewalk moves slightly to avoid walking into you. It proves you exist. Your mere existence caused them to alter their path. It's a nice feeling. After you die, no one has to get out of your way anymore.

Instead of school busing and prayer in schools, which are both controversial, why not a joint solution? Prayer in buses. Just drive these kids around all day and let them pray their fuckin' empty little heads off.

Lorena Bobbit only did what men do to each other all the time: She showed an asshole she meant business.

Americans are fucked. They've been bought off. And they came real cheap: a few million dirt bikes, camcorders, microwaves, cordless phones, digital watches, answering machines, jet skis, and sneakers with lights in them. You say you want a few items back from the Bill of Rights? Just promise the doofuses new gizmos.

I love it in a movie when they throw a guy off a cliff. I love it even when it's not a movie. No, especially when it's not a movie.

Owing to a basic programming flaw, many computer calculations, including mortgages and pensions, will be throw off by the arrival of the year 2000. It's because many computer programs use only the last two digits for calculating years. It will cost between 50 and 100 billion dollars to correct this mistake. I'm glad. I like anything that causes trouble.

Men don't show emotion, except rage, because it takes strength to show soft emotions. Most men don't have that kind of strength. They keep things inside. Then they kill someone.

Regarding Mount Rushmore: The Black Hills are sacred Indian ground. Imagine the creepy feeling of four leering European faces staring at your ancestors for eternity.

Who are all these people whose eyeglasses are attached to straps and bands around their necks? Please! Folks. Too precious. Hold your glasses, or set them down like the rest of us. Or perhaps, strange as it sounds, put them on. You need a dual correction? Get some bifocals.

HOUSES AND HOMES

housework/homework

houseboy/homeboy

housebreaker/homewrecker

housekeeper/homemaker

That thing you live in? Is it a house, or is it a home? Developers sell homes, but people buy houses.

Most people don't mind if you put 'em in a house. But under no circumstances do they want you to put 'em in a home. Unless it's a happy home. A happy home is not the same as a happy house. A happy house is one that's just been cleaned and painted. You'd be happy, too.

The madam Polly Adler once said, "A house is not a home." Of course, she meant a whorehouse is not a home. And it's not; no one would ever go to a whore home. Except a really old whore. That's where they go: The Old Whore's Home.

OPPOSITE-SAME-OPPOSITE

Sometimes the same words mean opposite things. Sometimes the opposite is true. Shock absorbers are called shocks. Slow down and slow up are interchangeable. Bad taste is tasteless. Sports fans say "turf" when they mean artificial turf. Something invaluable is very valuable. I'll bet you could care less. Or maybe you couldn't care less. Same difference. By the way, is it "from here on in" or "from here on out"?

INSIDE-OUT TALK

Here's something pretty stupid. You inflect these phrases the same way as the originals. It's inside-out talk! Tell your pals.

{ } Palsable celery

{ } The Arionese Syberation Limby

{ } Footday Night Monball

{ } Daise Don't Please the Eatsies

{ } A knocknical techout

{ } The New Bork Yockerknickers

{ } Beach the Combdanner

{ } Sylstoner Vallest

{ } Cronker Waltite

{ } The Unington of Washiversity

{ } Third Enkinders of the Close Count

{ } Kind Enclosures of the Third Count

{ } The Inhuldable Crelk

{ } Circy Flython's Pything Montus

{ } The Delaseverty Sixenty Philyers

WHAT'S MY MOTIVATION?

What's all this stuff about motivation? I say, if you need motivation, you probably need more than motivation. You probably need chemical intervention or brain surgery. Actually, if you ask me, this country could do with a little *less* motivation. The people who are causing all the trouble seem highly motivated to me. Serial killers, stock swindlers, drug dealers, Christian Republicans. I'm not sure motivation is always a good thing. You show me a lazy prick who's lying in bed all day, watching TV, only occasionally getting up to piss, and I'll show you a guy who's not causing any trouble.

THE GEORGE CARLIN BOOK CLUB— "We've Got Books Out the Ass"
Offer #2: Advice and Self-Help Titles

✖ *Where to Go for a Free Fuck*

✖ *Eat, Run, Stay Fit, and Die Anyway*

✖ *You Give Me Six Weeks and I'll Give You Some Bad Disease*

✖ *Why You Should Never Mambo with a Policeman*

✖ *The Stains in Your Shorts Can Indicate Your Future*

✖ *Earn Big Money by Sitting in Your Car Trunk*

☐ *Where to Take a Short Woman*

☐ *I Gave Up Hope and It Worked Just Fine*

☐ *Why You Should Never Yodel During an Electrical Storm*

☐ *Fill Your Life with Croutons*

☐ *Six Ways to Screw Up Before Breakfast*

☐ *I Suck, You Suck*

✖ *Reorganizing Your Pockets*

☐ *Where to Hide a Really Big Snot*

☐ *Why You Must Never Give Yourself a Neck Operation*

☐ *The Wrong Underwear Can Kill*

☐ *Now You Can Cure Cancer by Simply Washing Up*

☐ *Lightweight Summer Ensembles to Wear on the Toilet*

☐ *Why No One Should Be Allowed Out Anymore*

☐ *A Complete List of People Who Are Not Making Progress*

☐ *Where to Throw Up Secretly*

☐ *Ten Things No One Can Handle at All*

☐ *Why You Should Not Sit for More Than Six Weeks in Your Own Filth*

THE NEW ZODIAC

We need new zodiac signs. The old ones depict an obsolete world: the archer, the water bearer, and—talk about obsolete—the virgin. What we need are modern zodiac signs that represent today's reality: The Serial Rapist, the Lone Gunman, the Suicide Bomber, the

Paranoid Schizophrenic, the Transsexual Crackhead, the Money Launderer, the Disgruntled Postal Worker, the Diseased Homeless Veteran, the South American Drug Lord, the Third-Generation Welfare Recipient, the Human Immunodeficiency Virus, and . . . the Personal Trainer!

In case you're one of those people who doesn't relate well to the real world, here's a nice, safe zodiac for you: the Soccer Mom, the Sensitive Male, the Special Needs Child, the Role Model, the Overachiever, the Jogger, the Little Leaguer, the Recycler, the Anchorperson, the Codependent, the Domino's Delivery Boy, and . . . the Recovering Shopaholic.

GIVE A HOOT

I don't give a hoot. Not since 1959. That was the last one I gave. Wait! I think I gave a hoot in 1967. Just one. As a favor to a friend. But that was it. I'm not even sure I have any left. Frankly, I'd be afraid to look. I think I'm all out of hoots. If you want one, you're gonna have to find it on your own. Maybe you could rent a hoot. Or steal one. I'll bet by now there's a black market in hoots. Hot hoots. By the way, in addition to those who don't *give* a hoot, there are many others who will not *take* a hoot. Too proud. These are the same people who will not take any guff. But they might give you some lip.

BRING THE BODY CLOSER

I often hear otherwise intelligent people complaining about drivers who slow down when driving past a traffic accident. They curse them and call them "rubberneckers." I don't understand this at all. I am never in too big a hurry that I can't stop and watch someone else's suffering. The bigger the accident the better, as far as I'm concerned. I wanna see some guy whose neck is part of his gas tank. And if I can't see enough from my particular vantage point? I'll ask the policeman to bring the bodies over a little closer to my car. "Say, officer! Could you bring that twisted chap over here a little closer? I've never seen a man shaped quite like that." That's why the police are here: to protect, to serve, and to bring the bodies over a little closer to your car.

PAST-TENSE TV

I have a cable channel that shows old TV shows, but it shows them in different tenses from the originals. I don't know how they do it. Here's a sample:

Got Smart

Father Knew Best

It Was Left to Beaver

Daddy Had Had Room Made for Him

I Shall Have Been Loving Lucy

Car 54, Where Were You?

Had Gun, Would Have Traveled

What Had My Line Been?

I Have Had a Secret

That Had Been the Week That Had Been

ANYTHING BUT THE PRESENT

America has no now. We're reluctant to acknowledge the present. It's too embarrassing.

Instead, we reach into the past. Our culture is composed of sequels, reruns, remakes, revivals, reissues, re-releases, re-creations, re-enactments, adaptations, anniversaries, memorabilia, oldies radio, and nostalgia record collections. World War II has been refought on television so many times, the Germans and Japanese are now drawing residuals.

Of course, being essentially full of shit, we sometimes feel the need to dress up this past-preoccupation, as with pathetic references to reruns as "encore presentations."

Even instant replay is a form of token nostalgia: a brief visit to the immediate past for reexaminination, before slapping it onto a highlight video for further review and re-review on into the indefinite future.

Our "yestermania" includes fantasy baseball camps, where aging sad sacks pay money to catch baseballs thrown by men who were once their heroes. It is part of the fascination with sports memorabilia, a "memory industry" so lucrative it has attracted counterfeiters.

In this, the Age of Hyphens, we are truly retro-Americans.

And our television newscasts not only reflect this condition, they feed it. Everything they report is twisted into some reference to the past. If there's to be a summit meeting, you'll be told all about the last six summits; if there's a big earthquake, they'll do a story about big earthquakes of the past; if there's a mine disaster, you will hear about every mine disaster since the inception of mining. They're obsessed with looking back. I swear I actually heard this during a newscast, as the anchorman went to a commercial break: he said, "Still ahead, a look back." Honest.

"A look back: Hurricane Hugo, one year later." Why? The anniversary of the Exxon *Valdez* oil spill. For what reason? The anniversary of the Bay of Pigs, Pan Am Flight 103, the hostages in Iran, the fall of the Berlin Wall, V-J Day, V-E Day, Vietnam. Who gives a fuck?

Bugs Bunny's 50th birthday, Lassie's 55th, the Golden Jubilee of *Gone With the Wind*, the start of the Korean War, Barbie celebrates her 35th, the 25th anniversary of the New York blackout, Bambi turns 50. Shit, I didn't even like Bambi when I was supposed to, how much do I care now?

There's really no harm reviewing the past from time to time; knowing where you've been is part of knowing where you are, and all that happy horseshit. But the American media have an absolute fixation on this. They rob us of the present by insisting on the past. If they were able, I'm sure they would pay equal attention to the future. Trouble is, they don't have any film on it.

And so, on television news there is, oddly, very little emphasis on the present; on today's actual news. The present exists only in thirty-second stories built around eight-second sound bites. Remember, "sound bite" is their phrase. That's what they give you. Just a bite. No chewing, no digestion, no nourishment. Malnutrition.

Another way they avoid the present moment is to look ahead on their own schedules. The television news industry seems to revolve around what's coming next. "Still to come," "Just ahead," "Up next," "Coming up this half-hour," "More to come," "Stay with us," "Still ahead," "Also, later . . ."

They even preview what's going to happen as little as one hour later: During the "Five O'Clock News", the empty-headed prick who does the "Five O'Clock News" will suddenly say, "Here's a look at what's coming up on the 'Six O'Clock News.'" Then the empty-headed prick who does the "Six O'Clock News" will appear in shirtsleeves in the newsroom (to create the illusion of actual work) and tell you about several stories that the empty-headed prick who does the "Five O'Clock News" should already have told you about if he were really a newsman.

And so it goes, around the clock: On the "Five O'Clock News," they tell you about the "Six O'Clock News"; at six O'Clock, they tell you about eleven; at eleven, they plug the morning news; the morning man promos the noontime lady, and, sure enough, a little after noon, here comes that empty-headed prick from the "Five O'Clock News" to tell you what he's going to do . . . on the "Five O'Clock News."

You know, if a guy were paranoid, he might not be blamed for thinking that the people who run things don't want you dwelling too much on the present.

Because, keep in mind, the news media are not independent; they are a sort of bulletin board and public relations firm for the ruling class—the people who run things. Those who decide what news you will or will not hear are paid by, and tolerated purely at the whim of, those who hold economic power. If the parent corporation doesn't want you to know something, it won't be on the news. Period. Or, at the very least, it will be slanted to suit them, and then barely followed up.

Enjoy your snooze.

SOME FAVORITE OXYMORONS

assistant supervisor

new tradition

original copy

plastic glass

uninvited guest

highly depressed

live recording

authentic reproduction

partial cease-fire

limited lifetime guarantee

elevated subway

dry lake

true replica

forward lateral

standard options

iF i WERE iN CHARGE OF THE NETWORKS

I'm tired of television announcers, hosts, newscasters, and commentators, nibbling away at the English language, making obvious and ignorant mistakes.

If I were in charge of America's broadcast stations and networks, I would gather together all the people whose jobs include speaking to the public, and I would not let them out of the room until they had absorbed the following suggestions.

And I'm aware that media personalities are not selected on the basis of intelligence. I know that, and I try to make allowances for it. Believe me, I really try. But still . . .

There are some liberties taken with speech that I think require intervention, if only for my own sake. I won't feel right if this chance goes by, and I keep my silence.

The English word *forte*, meaning "specialty" or "strong point," is not pronounced "*for*-tay." Got that? It's pronounced "fort." The Italian word *forte*, used in music notation, is pronounced "*for*-tay," and it instructs the musician to play loud: "She plays the skin flute, and her forte [fort] is playing forte [*for*-tay]." Look it up. And don't give me that whiny shit, "*For*-tay is listed as the second preference." There's a reason it's second: because it's not *first*!

Irony deals with opposites; it has nothing to do with coincidence. If two baseball players from the same hometown, on different teams, receive the same uniform number, it is not ironic. It is a coincidence. If Barry Bonds attains lifetime statistics identical to his father's, it will not be ironic. It will be a coincidence. Irony is "a state of affairs that is the reverse of what was to be expected; a result opposite to and in mockery of the appropriate result." For instance:

If a diabetic, on his way to buy insulin, is killed by a runaway truck, he is the victim of an accident. If the truck was delivering sugar, he is the victim of an oddly poetic coincidence. But if the truck was delivering insulin, ah! Then he is the victim of an irony.

If a Kurd, after surviving a bloody battle with Saddam Hussein's army and a long, difficult escape through the mountains, is crushed and killed by a parachute drop of humanitarian aid, that, my friend, is irony writ large.

Darryl Stingley, the pro football player, was paralyzed after a brutal hit by Jack Tatum. Now Darryl Stingley's son plays football, and if the son should become paralyzed while playing, it will not be ironic. It will be coincidental. If Darryl Stingley's son paralyzes someone else, that will be closer to ironic. If he paralyzes Jack Tatum's son that will be precisely ironic.

I'm tired of hearing *prodigal* being used to mean "wandering, given to running away or leaving and returning." The parable in the Book of Luke tells of a son who squanders his father's money. *Prodigal* means "recklessly wasteful or extravagant." And if you say popular usage has changed that, I say, fuck popular usage!

The phrase *sour grapes* does not refer to jealousy or envy. Nor is it related to being a sore loser. It deals with the rationalization of failure to attain a desired end. In the original

fable by Aesop, "The Fox and the Grapes," when the fox real-
izes he cannot leap high enough to reach the grapes, he ratio-
nalizes that even if he had gotten them, they would probably
have been sour anyway. Rationalization. That's all sour grapes
means. It doesn't deal with jealousy or sore losing. Yeah, I
know, you say, "Well, many people are using it that way, so the
meaning is changing." And I say, "Well many people are really fuckin' stupid, too, shall we just adopt all their standards?"

Strictly speaking, *celibate* does not mean not having sex,
it means not being married. No wedding. The practice of
refraining from sex is called *chastity* or *sexual abstinence.* No
fucking. Priests don't take a vow of celibacy, they take a vow
of chastity. Sometimes referred to as the "no-nookie clause."

And speaking of sex, the *Immaculate Conception* does
not mean Jesus was conceived in the absence of sex. It
means Mary was conceived without Original Sin. That's all
it has ever meant. And according to the tabloids, Mary is
apparently the only one who can make such a claim. The
Jesus thing is called *virgin birth.*

Proverbial is now being used to describe things that
don't appear in proverbs. For instance, "the proverbial drop
in the bucket" is incorrect because "a drop in the bucket" is
not a proverb, it's a metaphor. You wouldn't say, "as welcome as a turd in the proverbial punchbowl," or "as cold as
the proverbial nun's box," because neither refers to a
proverb. The former is a metaphor, the latter is a simile.

Momentarily means *for* a moment, not *in* a moment. The word for "in a moment" is *presently*. "I will be there presently, Dad, and then, after pausing momentarily, I will kick you in the nuts."

No other option and *no other alternative* are redundant. The words *option* and *alternative* already imply otherness. "I had no option, Mom, I got this huge erection because there was no alternative." This rule is not optional; the alternative is to be wrong.

You should not use *criteria* when you mean *criterion* for the same reason that you should not use *criterion* when you mean *criteria*. These is my only criterions.

A *light-year* is a measurement of distance, not time. "It will take light years for young basketball players to catch up with the number of women Wilt Chamberlain has fucked," is a scientific impossibility. Probably in more ways than one.

An *acronym* is not just any set of initials. It applies only to those that are pronounced as words. MADD, DARE, NATO, and UNICEF are acronyms. FBI, CIA, and KGB are not. They're just pricks.

I know I'm fighting a losing battle with this one, but I refuse to surrender: Collapsing a building with explosives is not an *implosion*. An *implosion* is a very specific scientific phenomenon. The collapsing of a building with explosives is the collapsing of a building with explosives. The explosives explode, and the building collapses inwardly. That is not an implosion. It is an inward collapsing of a building, following a series of smaller explosions designed to make it collapse inwardly. Period. Fuck you!

Here's another pointless, thankless objection I'd like to register. I say it that way, because I know you people and your goddamn "popular usage" slammed the door on this one a long time ago. But here goes anyway:

A *cop out* is not an excuse, not even a weak one; it is an admission of guilt. When someone "cops a plea," he admits guilt to some charge, in exchange for better treatment. He has "copped out." When a guy says, "I didn't get to fuck her because I reminded her of her little brother," he is making an excuse. But if he says, "I didn't get to fuck her because I'm an unattractive schmuck," he is copping out. The trouble arises when an excuse contains a small amount of self-incriminating truth.

This one is directed to the sports people: You are destroying a perfectly good figure of speech: "Getting the monkey off one's back" does not mean breaking a losing streak. It refers only to ending a dependency. That's all. The monkey represents a strong yen. A losing streak does not compare even remotely. Not in a literary sense and not in real life.

Here's one you hear from the truly dense: "The proof is in the pudding." Well, the proof is not in the pudding; the rice and the raisins are in the pudding. The proof of the pudding is in the eating. In this case, proof means "test." The same is true of "the exception that proves (tests) the rule."

An *eye for an eye* is not a call for revenge, it is an argument for fairness. In the time of the Bible, it was standard to take a life in exchange for an eye. But the Bible said, No, the punishment should fit the crime. Only an eye for an eye, nothing more. It is not vindictive, it is mitigatory.

Don't make the same mistake twice seems to indicate three mistakes, doesn't it? First you make the mistake. Then you make the same mistake. Then you make the same mistake twice. If you simply say, "Don't make the same mistake," you'll avoid the first mistake.

Unique needs no modifier. *Very unique, quite unique, more unique, real unique, fairly unique,* and *extremely unique* are wrong, and they mark you as dumb. Although certainly not unique.

Healthy does not mean "healthful." Healthy is a condition, healthful is a property. Vegetables aren't healthy, they're dead. No food is healthy. Unless you have an eggplant that's doing push-ups. Push-ups are healthful.

There is no such thing or word as *kudo. Kudos* is a singular noun meaning praise, and it is pronounced *kyoo*-dose. There is also a plural form, spelled the same, but pronounced *kyoo*-doze. Please stop telling me, "So-and-so picked up another kudo today."

Race, creed, or color is wrong. Race and color, as used in this phrase, describe the same property. And "creed" is a stilted, outmoded way of saying "religion." Leave this tired phrase alone; it has lost its usefulness. Besides, it reeks of insincerity no matter who uses it.

As of yet is simply stupid. As yet, I've seen no progress on this one, but of course I'm speaking as of now.

Here's one you can win money on in a bar if you're within reach of the right reference book: *Chomping at the bit* and *old stomping ground* are incorrect. Some Saturday afternoon when you're gettin' bombed on your old stamping ground, you'll be champing at the bit to use this one.

Sorry to sound so picky, folks, but I listen to a lot of radio and TV, and these things have bothered me for a long time.

VIEWERS, BEWARE!

Television newscasters often warn viewers that something they're going to show might upset people: "Be warned that this next film clip is very graphic, and contains explicit language, so you might want to consider if you want to see it, or if it is suitable for your children." Imagine! Explicit and graphic! Here are the definitions of those words according to *Webster's Third New International Dictionary*:

Explicit: Characterized by full, clear expression; being without vagueness or ambiguity.

Graphic: Marked by clear and lively description or striking imaginative power. Sharply outlined or delineated.

So what is the problem here? Why do they feel it necessary to warn people against the possibility of seeing something clear, sharply outlined, unambiguous, and with striking imaginative power?

THE "PRE-" EPIDEMIC

Preboard, prescreen, prerecord, pretaped, preexisting, preorder, preheat, preplan, pretest, precondition, preregister. In nearly all of these cases you can drop the "pre" and not change the meaning of the word.

"The suicide film was not prescreened by the school." No, of course not. It was screened.

"You can call and prequalify for a loan over the phone. Your loan is preapproved." Well, if my loan is approved before I call then no approval is necessary. The loan is simply available.

NAME IT LIKE IT IS

The words *Fire Department* make it sound like they're the ones who are starting the fires, doesn't it? It should be called the "Extinguishing Department." We don't call the police the "Crime Department." Also, the "Bomb Squad" sounds like a terrorist gang. The same is true of *wrinkle cream.* Doesn't it sound like it causes wrinkles? And why would a doctor prescribe pain pills? I already *have* pain! I need relief pills!

MORE FAVORITE OXYMORONS

mandatory options

mutual differences

nondairy creamer

open secret

resident alien

silent alarm

sports sedan

wireless cable

mercy killing

lethal assistance (Contra aid)

business ethics

friendly fire

genuine veneer

full-time day care

death benefits

holy war

SUPER-CELEB KICKS BUCKET

I dread the deaths of certain super-celebrities. Not because I care about them, but because of all the shit I have to endure on television when one of them dies. All those tributes and retrospectives. And the bigger the personality, the worse it is.

For instance, imagine the crap we'll have to endure on TV when Bob Hope dies. First of all, they'll show clips from all his old road movies with Bing Crosby, and you can bet that some news anchor asshole will turn to the pile of clothing next to him and say, "Well, Tami, I imagine Bob's on the Road to Heaven now."

Then there'll be clips of all those funny costumes he wore on his TV specials, including the hippie sketch, where they'll show him saying,

"Far out, man, far out!" They'll show him golfing with dead presidents, kissing blonde bombshells, and entertaining troops in every war since we beat the shit out of the Peloponnesians. And at some point, a seventy-year-old veteran will choke up, and say, "I just missed seein' him at Iwo, 'cause I got my legs blowed off. He's quite a guy."

Ex-presidents (including the dead ones) will line up four abreast to tell us what a great American he was; show-business perennials will desert golf courses from Palm Springs to O.J.'s lawn to lament sadly as how this time, "Bob hooked one into the woods"; and, regarding his talent, a short comedian in a checkered hat will speak reverently about "Hope's incredible timing."

And this stuff will be on every single newscast day and night for a week. There'll be special one-hour salutes on "Good Morning America," the "Today" show, and "CBS This Morning." Ted Koppel will ask Henry Kissinger if it's true Bob Hope actually shortened some of our wars by telling jokes close to the frontlines. CNN will do a series of expanded "Show Biz Todays." One of the cable channels will do a one-week marathon of his movies. And it goes without saying that NBC will put together a three-hour, prime-time special called "Thanks for the Memories," but at the last minute they'll realize Bob Hope's audience skews older, and sell it to CBS.

Then there'll be the funeral, carried live on the Dead Celebrity Channel, with thousands of grotesque acne-ridden fans seeking autographs from all the show-business clowns who dug out their best black golfing outfits to attend "one of the hottest burials to hit this town in decades"—*Variety.*

And all this shit will go on for weeks and weeks and weeks. Until Milton Berle dies. And then it will start all over again. I dare not even contemplate Frank Sinatra and Ronald Reagan.

KEEP IT—WE DON'T WANT IT

Don't you get tired of celebrities who explain their charity work by saying they feel they have to"give something back." I don't feel that way. I didn't take nothin'. You can search my house; I didn't take a thing. Everything I got, I worked for, and it was given to me freely. I also paid taxes on it. Late! I paid late. But I paid. You celebrity people wanna give something back? How about giving back half the money? Or a couple of those houses? And you dickwads who collect cars? How about giving back 50 or 60 of them? Or maybe, if you people really want to give something back, you could let go of a little of that arrogance.

DESERVING CHARITIES

For my part, I like to work quietly in the background, helping my preferred charities raise money. If you'd like to help too, here are just a few you might consider.

✖ St. Anthony's Shelter for the Recently All Right

✖ The Christian Haven for the Chronically Feisty

✖ The Committee to Keep Something-or-Other from Taking Place

✖ The Center for Research into the Heebie Jeebies

✖ Free Hats for Fat People

✖ The Task Force for Better Pancakes

✖ The Home for the Visually Unpleasant

✖ The State Hospital for Those Who Felt All Right About a Year Ago

{ } The Committee to Challenge the Height Requirements of Mailmen

{ } The Beverly Hills Chamber of Poor Taste

{ } The Alliance of People Who Don't Know What's Next

{ } The Downtown Mission for the Permanently Disheveled

{ } The Malibu Home for the Unimportant

{ } The Nook for Needy Nuns

{ } Children of Parents with Bad Teeth

{ } The Rochester Home for Soreheads

{ } The League of People Who Should Know Better

{ } Hors d'Oeuvres for Bangladesh

{ } The Brotherhood of Real Creeps

{ } The Committee to Remove the "Bah" from "Sis Boom Bah"

PEOPLE I CAN DO WITHOUT

{ } A stranger on the train who wants to tell me about his bowel movements.

{ } People who whistle cowboy songs during a funeral.

{ } Anyone who refers to Charles Manson as "Chuck."

{ } A tall man with a Slavic accent wearing a bow tie of human flesh.

{ } Any couple who owns "his and hers" rectal thermometers.

{ } A girl whose wallet contains nude photos of Sam Donaldson or Yassir Arafat.

{ } A man with a tattoo that shows Joey Buttafuco dancing the Lambada with Leona Helmsley.

{ } Any man who can ingest a quart of vegetable soup through his nose in one long suck.

{ } A priest with an eye patch and a limp who's selling pieces of the cross.

{ } Any guy named Dogmeat whose body has over six square feet of scar tissue.

{ } Anyone who takes off work on Ted Bundy's birthday.

{ } A man with gold front teeth who wants to play stud poker on the floor of the bus station men's room.

{ } A crying woman with a harpoon gun entering a sports bar.

{ } Anyone who gets plastic surgery in an attempt to look more intelligent.

{ } A man with one cloven hoof who wants to give my daughter a hysterectomy.

{ } A seventy-year-old man wearing gag underpants that say "We visited the Grassy Knoll."

{ } Any man with a birthmark shaped like a hypodermic needle.

{ } Any woman who repeatedly gives me a high five during sex.

{ } A cross-eyed man in a New Year's hat reciting "Casey at the Bat" in Latin.

- Anyone who receives e-mail from Willard Scott.

- A man who plunges a bone-handled carving fork through his neck in order to get my attention.

- Anyone with three nostrils.

- A bag lady wearing over 200 garments, including nine separate hats.

- Any man who tries to pierce his ear with an electric can opener.

- A retarded twelve-year-old who carries more than six books of matches.

- Any man who gives himself a Harvey Wallbanger enema. On the rocks.

- Any person bleeding from three orifices who wants me to cosign on a loan.

- A homely, flat-chested woman wearing a Foxy Lady T-shirt.

SPACED OUT

You know something I could really do without? The Space Shuttle. Why don't these people go out and get real jobs? It's the same shit over and over. They get delayed, they blast off, they get in orbit, something breaks, they fix it, the President says hello, Mission Control wakes them up with a song no one has listened to in twenty years, the science experiment placed on board by the third-graders of Frog Balls, Tennessee, is a big success, and bla bla bla. It's time to end this shit. Besides, it's irresponsible. The last thing we should be doing is sending our grotesquely distorted DNA out into space.

EXPRESSIONS I QUESTION

IN THE PRIVACY OF YOUR OWN HOME. As opposed to what? The privacy of someone else's home? You have no privacy in someone else's home; that's why you got your own home.

DOWN THE PIKE. "He was the meanest guy ever to come down the pike." Fine. What about guys who come *up* the pike? Not everyone lives "north of the pike." Some guys have to come *up* the pike, and they're really mean, because nobody mentions them at all. And what about a guy who doesn't even *use* the pike? He arrives on Amtrak! "Boy, he was the meanest guy ever to arrive on Amtrak." Doesn't sound right.

LIKE A BAT OUT OF HELL. We say some guy was "goin' like a bat outta Hell." How do we know how fast a bat would leave Hell? Maybe he would leave real slow. In fact, why should we assume that a bat would even want to leave Hell? Maybe he likes it there. Maybe Hell is just right for a bat. Maybe it's bat heaven. And now that we're on this subject, how do we know Hell has bats in the first place? What would a bat be doin' in Hell? Usually a bat is in the belfry. Why would he want to split his time between two places? Then again, maybe that's why he's in such a hurry to leave Hell. He's due back at the belfry.

Why do we say **OUT LIKE A LIGHT**? The primary function of a light is to be lit, not to be out. Why choose a light to represent the concept of being out? Why not, "*On* like a light?" The same is true of **DROPPING LIKE FLIES**; the wrong quality is being emphasized. Flies are known for flying, not dropping. And let's forget **METEORIC RISE**. Meteors don't rise, they fall.

You can talk until you're blue in the face, etc. etc. Well, you can't talk until you're blue in the face. In order to talk, you need oxygen. Blueness of the face is caused by a lack of oxygen. So, if you're blue in the face, you probably stopped talking a long time ago. You might be making some gestures. In fact, if you're running out of oxygen, I would imagine you're making quite a number of gestures. And rather flamboyant ones at that.

When we point out someone's lack of popularity, especially a politician's, we sometimes say, He couldn't get elected dog catcher. First of all, since when do they elect dog catchers? I've never seen one on the ballot, have you? The last time you were in the voting booth, did it say, "President, Vice President, Dog Catcher?" No. And why do they imply that getting elected dog catcher would be easy? I think it would be hard. A lot of people have dogs; they wouldn't vote for you. And many of the people who don't have dogs still like them. I should think it would be quite difficult to get elected dog catcher.

One thing leads to another. Not always. Sometimes one thing leads to the same thing. Ask an addict.

The pen is mightier than the sword needs to be updated. It's overdue. It should have been changed much earlier in the twentieth century to, "The typewriter is mightier than the machine gun." But at this point is should probably read, "The word processor is mightier than the particle-beam weapon."

Unidentified person. What exactly is an "unidentified person"? Doesn't everyone have an identity? Maybe they mean he's a person they can't identify. But that would make him an "unidentifiable person." I guess if nothing else, he could always be referred to as "that guy we can't identify."

OPEN A CAN OF WORMS. Why would you have to open it? Are there really sealed cans of worms? Who sealed them? Worms are usually put in a can *after* it has been opened, and emptied of something else, like corn or pumpkin meat. Uncover a can of worms, maybe. But not open.

WILD AND WOOLLY. Whenever I hear something described as wild and woolly, I always wonder where the woolly part comes in. Wild I understand. But woolly? I have some sweaters that are woolly, but they're kind of conservative. Not wild at all.

IN THE WRONG PLACE AT THE WRONG TIME. How can this be? Shouldn't it be, "In the *right* place at the wrong time?" If a guy gets hit by a stray bullet, he is in the right place (where his day's activities have taken him) at the wrong time (when a bullet is passing by). If it were the wrong place, the bullet wouldn't have been there.

IN THE RIGHT PLACE AT THE RIGHT TIME is also questionable. Let's say a guy wins a prize for being a bank's millionth customer. All you really have to say is, "He was in the right place." After all, it *had* to be the right time. That's the only time they were giving away the prize. If it hadn't been the right time, it wouldn't have been the right place. Twenty minutes later the bank wouldn't be "the right place" anymore.

YOU NEVER KNOW. Not true. Sometimes you know.

YOU DON'T HAVE TO BE A ROCKET SCIENTIST implies that rocket scientists are somehow smart. How smart can they be? They build machines that travel thousands of miles to drop fire and radiation on people. That doesn't sound smart to me.

THE OLDEST TRICK IN THE BOOK. Sometimes in the movies, when the bad guy is holding a gun on the good guy, the good guy says, "It won't work, Scarfelli. My men are right behind you with their guns drawn." And the bad guy says, "You can't fool me, Murdoch, that's the oldest trick in the book." Well, exactly what book are these guys talking about? Have you ever seen a book with a bunch of tricks in it? Magic tricks maybe, but I don't think the thing with the guns would be in there, do you? A prostitute might have a book of tricks, but once again, probably no mention of the two guys with the guns. And anyway, even if there really were a book with a lot of tricks in it, how would you know which trick was the oldest? They were all printed at the same time. You'd have to say, "You can't fool me, Murdoch, that's the trick that appears earliest in the book." But that's not good movie dialogue, is it?

When they say someone is NOT GOING TO WIN ANY POPULARITY CONTESTS, what popularity contests are they talking about? I've never heard of these contests. Where do they have them? And who wins? Whoever is winning these popularity contests can't be that popular. You never hear about them.

YOU COULD HEAR A PIN DROP. Well, you can't hear a pin drop. Not even a bowling pin. When a pin is dropping, it's just floating through the air. There's very little noise. You might be able to hear a pin land but certainly not drop.

WORDS AND PHRASES WE SHOULD HAVE

re-go = to return somewhere

un-park = to drive away

de-have = to lose something

re-get = to find it again

firmth = firmness

pocketry = a garment's pockets

way much: "Ice cream tastes way much better than sewage."

a lotta buncha: "I only slept with her once, and now I got a lotta buncha crabs.

a very lot: "The gold-plated dildos cost a very lot more than the rubber ones."

a whole much: "I love you a whole much."

real pretty good: "I'm real pretty good at math."

very pretty good: "But I'm very pretty good at history."

extremely not bad: "This prune cake is extremely not bad."

very thank you: "Oh, thank you. Very, very thank you!"

yesternight: "I couldn't get to sleep yesternight."

last morning: "So I was real tired last morning."

SOME FAVORITE REDUNDANCIES

added bonus

exactly right

closed fist

future potential

inner core

money-back refund

seeing the sights

true fact

revert back

safe haven

prior history

young children

time period

sum total

end result

temper tantrum

ferryboat

free gift

bare naked

combined total

unique individual

potential hazard

joint cooperation

POPULAR BELIEFS

There are many popular beliefs rooted in familiar expressions and sayings that simply aren't true.

EVERYTHING COMES IN THREES. Not true. In reality, everything comes in ones. Sometimes, when three "ones" come in a row, it *seems* like everything comes in threes. By the way, in medieval times it was widely believed that everything came in twenty-sixes. They were wrong, too. It just took them longer to recognize a pattern.

People say when you die, **YOU CAN'T TAKE IT WITH YOU.** Well, that depends on what it is. If it's your dark blue suit, you can certainly take it with you. In fact, not only can you take it with you, you can probably put some things in the pockets.

YOU LEARN SOMETHING NEW EVERY DAY. Actually, you learn something old every day. Just because you just learned it, doesn't mean it's new. Other people already knew it. Columbus is a good example of this.

THE SKY'S THE LIMIT. Well, how can the sky be the limit? The sky never ends. What kind of a limit is that? The Earth is the limit. You dig a hole and what do you keep getting? More earth. The Earth's the limit.

YOU GET WHAT YOU PAY FOR. Clearly this is not true. Have you been shopping lately? Only a naive person would believe that you get what you pay for. In point of fact, if you check your purchases carefully, you'll find that you get whatever they feel like giving you. And if corporations get any more powerful, you soon might not even get that.

TOMORROW IS ANOTHER DAY. Not true. Today is another day. We have no idea what tomorrow is going to be. It might turn out to *be* another day, but we can't be sure. If it happens, I'll be the first to say so. But, you know what? By that time, it'll be today again.

NICE GUYS FINISH LAST. Not true. Studies have shown that, on the average, nice guys finish third in a field of six. Actually, short guys finish last. By the way, in medieval times it was widely believed that nice guys finished twenty-sixth. You can see how limited those people were.

IF YOU'VE SEEN ONE, YOU'VE SEEN 'EM ALL. Do we even have to talk about this one? This should be obvious. If you've seen one, you've seen one. If you've seen them all, *then* you've seen them all. I don't understand how this one even got started.

THOSE WERE THE DAYS. No. Those were the nights! Think back. Weren't the nights better? Days you had to work. Nights you went to parties, danced, drank, got laid. "Those were the nights!"

THERE'S NO SUCH THING AS A FREE LUNCH. What about when you eat at home? I don't pay when I eat lunch at home–it's free! Sometimes I'll leave a tip, but basically, it's a free lunch. Yes, I know we had to buy the food at the store. But as the Zen Buddhists say, The Food Is Not the Lunch.

YOU PAYS YOUR MONEY, AND YOU TAKES YOUR CHOICE. I think what I said earlier still applies: You pays your money and you takes whatever they jolly well give you. Actually, when you get right down to it, you pays your money and you *loses* your money.

EVERYBODY HAS HIS PRICE. Not so. Would you believe there are millions of people who do not have their price? Thanks to a government mixup, many people have their neighbor's price.

THEY DON'T MAKE 'EM LIKE THEY USED TO. Actually they do make 'em like they used to, they just don't sell 'em anymore. They make 'em, and they keep 'em!

TWO WRONGS DON'T MAKE A RIGHT. Well, it just so happens that two wrongs do make a right. Not only that, but as the number of wrongs increases, the whole thing goes up exponentially. So that while two wrongs make one right, and four wrongs make two rights, it actually takes sixteen wrongs to make three rights, and 256 wrongs to make four rights. It seems to me that anyone who is stringing together more that 256 wrongs needs counseling, not mathematics.

IF IT'S NOT ONE THING, IT'S ANOTHER. Not always. Sometimes if it's not one thing, not only is it not another, but it turns out to be something else altogether.

YOU CAN'T WIN THEM ALL. Not true. Believe it or not, there is a man in Illinois who, so far, has won them all. But don't get too excited; it has also been discovered that under certain circumstances it is possible to lose them all. By the way, there is no record of anyone having tied them all.

YOU CAN'T HAVE IT BOTH WAYS. That depends on how intimately you know the other person. Maybe you can't have it both ways at once, but if you've got a little time, you can probably have it six or seven ways.

THINGS HAVE TO GET BETTER, THEY CAN'T GET ANY WORSE. This is an example of truly faulty logic. Just because things can't get any worse, is no reason to believe they have to get better. They might just stay the same. And, by the way, who says things can't get any worse? For many people, things get worse and worse and worse.

NOBODY EVER SAID LIFE WAS FAIR. Not so. I specifically remember as I was growing up, at least twelve different people, telling me life was fair. One person put it this way: "Life, you will find, is fair, George." Oddly enough, all twelve of those people died before the age of twenty-seven.

IT TAKES TWO TO TANGO. Sounds good, but simple reasoning will reveal that actually it takes only one to tango. It takes two to tango together, maybe, but one person is certainly capable of tangoing on his own. By the way, in medieval times it was widely believed that it took twenty-six to tango.

THERE'S A SUCKER BORN EVERY MINUTE, AND TWO TO TAKE HIM. This may have been true in the past, but now, if you adjust for the increased population base, birth control, and the so-called moral decline, not only are there five suckers born every minute, there are now fifty-three to take him.

LIFE IS SHORT. Sorry. Life is not short, it's just that since everything else lasts so long—mountains, rivers, stars, planets—life seems short. Actually life lasts just the right amount of time. Until you die. Death on the other hand, is short.

WHAT YOU DON'T KNOW WON'T HURT YOU. Why don't we just ask Abe Lincoln and John Kennedy about this one.

FROZEN MEXICAN DINNER

Sometimes on television they tell you to buy a frozen Mexican dinner. Well, it sounds like a good idea, but actually, before you take him out to dinner, I should think it would be a good idea to bring him in the house and let him warm up a little. A frozen Mexican probably wouldn't be thinking mainly about food. By the way, isn't Mexico a warm-weather country?

MORE FAVORITE REDUNDANCIES

total abstinence

subject matter

honest truth

join together

general public

harbinger of things to come

new initiative

audible gasp

advance warning

execution-style killing

future plans

gather together

Jewish synagogue

lag behind

manual dexterity

occasional irregularity

outer rim

plan ahead

basic fundamentals

first time ever

personal friend

shrug one's shoulders

WATCH YOUR MOUTH

BEWARE OF AGGRAVATING SPEAKERS

I am easily annoyed by people's speech habits, and I regard certain words and phrases as warnings to break off contact. In the interest of maintaining good mental health, I avoid the following people:

Those who can't resist saying, "God forbid" each time they mention the possibility of an accident or death, even though they don't believe in God.

People who say "God rest his soul" following the mention of a dead person, even if they hated the person and don't believe in God. These are the same ones who say "knock wood" and really mean it. Sometimes they'll even glance around halfheartedly for something to knock on, before giving up and just standing there like the morons they are.

And speaking of morons, can't we somehow prevent adults from using words like *tushie, boo-boo* and *no-no,* when speaking to grown-ups? Why don't we just send these people to their rooms without supper? Tell them there's not gonna be any yummy in their tummy. And while we're at it, let's include all those colorful risk-takers who actually use *heck* and *darn* for emphasis. What the fuck is this, 1850?

I also think we'd be better off if we could eliminate anyone who has a "can-do" attitude, or is referred to as "take-charge," "all-business," or "no-nonsense." Have these people sedated.

And let's include the ones who describe themselves as "goal-oriented." Please. Leave me alone.

And the ones who tell you, "I'm a people person." Yeah? Me too. Fuck people!

And what about these guys who have no job and say to you, "Are they keepin' ya busy?" I happen to resent even the assumption that there are people who have the authority to keep me busy. Least of all do I appreciate it from some guy who doesn't seem to have a whole lot to do, himself.

And let's punish every homely man who ever thought it was clever to say, "I'm not just another pretty face."

And I think it's time to start slapping around these people who can't tell a simple story without repeatedly saying, "Ya know what I'm sayin'?" Here I am, trying to listen to the guy, and he's a person who is constantly checking on how he's doing.

"Bla, bla, bla. Ya know what I'm sayin'?"

No, the question is not, do I know what you're saying, the

question is, do you know what you're saying? You follow me on that?

I'm also getting tired of *arguably*. It's weak. It tries to have things both ways. Take a stand!

And here are some jock/sports-fan adjectives that should be outlawed: Listening to a sports call-in radio station for about an hour, you will be amazed at the number of times you hear the following words: incredible, unbelievable, tremendous, outstanding, big, huge, large, major, and key. Do these guys sound like maybe someone's penis size is on their minds?

I can also do without people who tell me that something—anything—is either "the name of the game" or "what it's all about." Oh it is, huh? Well, fuck you!

And let's lose these guys who think it's cute to say, "Ouch!" when someone delivers a small put-down.

BEWARE ALSO OF THE PRETENTIOUS AND ARROGANT SPEAKER

People who refer to themselves as "yours truly." What kind of grandiose crap is this? Some even speak of themselves in the third person. Athletes and entertainers are big on this demented shit: "I'm gonna do what's right for Leon Spinks!" I think people like this are mentally ill. And you can include those very special people who use the royal "we."

I also instantly dismiss anyone who tells me that some other person "has class," "is classy," or "is a class act," the last of these being the most arrogant. What these speakers are telling you is that since they are among the few people who recognize class, it is their obligation to point it out to sorry-ass folks like you. If you manage to listen to them just a little longer, you'll find that they're completely full of shit.

This is the same type of person who uses the word "tasty" when referring to music.

The above sort of reference to class is of the same order of arrogance as the phrases "not too shabby," "he's no dummy," "I give him high marks," "he's got his head on straight," and "he really showed me something." All of these phrases reek of presumed superiority.

And just when I thought all those precious twerps were about to stop saying, "Not to worry," and "By the by," along came "What say you?" and "At the end of the day" to deepen my suffering. "At the end of the day" is probably the most pretentious expression to come along since the "moi-ciao" crowd descended on us.

"Just a tad" has a phony ring to it. So does "just a skosh."

And be on the alert for anyone who tells you that something they did was "life-affirming." Some celebrity said he quit doing his TV show because "it stopped being life-affirming." Hey, Skeezix, when you finish affirming your life, get over here and give my dick a coupla yanks.

And can't we figure out something evil to do to these people who call themselves "survivors"? Such self-regard!

"I'm a survivor."

"Good. We'll be sure to tell everyone at your funeral that you're a fuckin' survivor."

This one is almost too easy: guys who can't leave a room without saying, "I'm outta here." You know what I say to them? "Good! Stay the fuck outta here!"

There are also certain reckless people in this country who are abusing "ongoing" and "early on." Leave these terms alone, please. They mark you as a counterfeit. "Early on" has faux poetic aspirations, and "ongoing" has only a very narrow area where it is distinctly appropriate.

And some of these "ongoing" felons are the same ones who have vandalized the phrase "even as we speak." First they shortened it to "as we speak." Then they started using it every four minutes or so. Even as I write this, my pissed-off-edness is ongoing.

And fuck all the asshole people who say, "God bless," and then don't bother to complete the sentence. Who they are, I haven't the slightest. But, if I were God, I would not honor such a request. Anyway, enjoy.

More general lame overused expressions for which the users ought to be slain:

〔 〕 From the git-go

〔 〕 It works for me.

〔 〕 You gotta love it.

〔 〕 Go get 'em, tiger!

〔 〕 Sounds like a plan.

〔 〕 You know the drill.

〔 〕 Get with the program.

〔 〕 Take no prisoners.

〔 〕 None of the above

{ } Up close and personal

{ } The whole nine yards

{ } May be hazardous to your health

{ } The Rodney Dangerfield of . . .

{ } Cut to the chase.

{ } Deal with it.

{ } Clean up your act.

{ } Bottom line

{ } Wannabe

{ } Been there, done that.

{ } Fifteen minutes of fame

{ } Joined at the hip

{ } Flavor of the month

{ } It's not over till it's over.

{ } Don't try this at home.

{ } Easy for you to say.

{ } Separated at birth.

✖ I'm mad as hell and, etc.

{ } Just when you thought it was safe . . .

{ } Humungous

{ } In your face

{ } Lean and mean

❏ Check it out.

❏ Doesn't take a rocket scientist

❏ Do a number

✖ Couch potato

✖ What's wrong with this picture?

✖ Or what?

❏ Born again

❏ Trash talk

❏ I love it!

❏ Go ballistic

❏ In your dreams

❏ I hate when that happens.

❏ Don't give up your day job.

❏ Tough act to follow

❏ No brainer

❏ Street smart

❏ I mean that in the nicest way.

❏ No biggie

❏ Tell us how you *really* feel.

❏ That's why he gets the big bucks.

PROBLEM!

I have a problem with guys who say "No problem." The phrase has outlasted its usefulness, and, more alarming, it has almost completely replaced "You're welcome."

"Thank you for carrying those ten bodies downstairs and putting them in the lime pit with all the dead puppies."

"No problem."

And, of course, there are the really cool guys who abbreviate it:

"No prob!"

These are the same dipshits who say "bod" for body and "bud" for buddy.

And let's not forget the very special, very precious ones who can't resist saying "No problemo!"

Don't you love these guys? "No problemo!" Same ones who say "Correcta-mundo," and "Exacta-mundo." Mock foreign.

And "moi"! Of course, *moi* being a real word makes the person seem even more pretentious; same category as the "ciao" crowd.

I could really do without non-Italians who lay a worldly, continental "Ciao," on me and then wander off to hitchhike home. They're right up there with the freckle-faced, redheaded lads who belch up huge, moist beer clouds in my face and then insist on calling me "amigo."

YOU'RE GODDAMN RIGHT!

There are many replies you can make when you hear a statement you agree with. A real old-timer says, "You're darn tootin'!"

"I've noticed your granddaughter's nipples stiffen up when I moisten my lips."

"You're darn tootin'!"

In my father's day it was, "You can say that again."

"Hey, Dad, Mom's ass is starting to sag real bad."

"You can say that again."

When I was a kid we said, "I'm wise" or "I'm hip."

"Man, your sister gives a good blow job!"

"I'm hip."

Eventually, we grew tired of these expressions. Now there are new ones, and I'm getting tired of them, too. Examples:

"I hear ya."

"Wonderful. And are you picking me up visually as well?"

"Tell me about it."

"I just did."

"I heard that!"

"Oh, really? Well, isn't that exciting! What is this, a hearing test? Did I wander into a Beltone commercial? Of course you heard it, ya fuckin' nimrod, I'm standin' right next to ya! I'm gonna wander over here a little farther away. BLOW ME!!! By any chance, did ya hear that?"

"You got that right."

"What are you, Alex Trebek? Oh. Well, in that case, I'll take 'Bodies of Water' for $300."

EVEN MORE FAVORITE REDUNDANCIES

bond together

close proximity

ATM machine

PIN number

coequal

common bond

small minority

serious crisis

personal belongings

security guard

time clock

foreign imports

exact same

continue on

focus in

convicted felon

past experience

consensus of opinion

finished product

schoolteacher

linger on

THE PRIMITIVE SERGEANT

There was a first time for everything. At some point, every custom, every practice, every ritual had to be explained to people for the first time. It must have been tricky, especially in primitive societies.

For instance, the first human sacrifice. Not of the enemy, but the first ritual killing of a member of your own tribe. Someone had to announce it to the people. Someone with authority, but probably not the top guy. A sergeant. A primitive sergeant, addressing a band of early cave people—hunters, gatherers, whatever—explaining the human sacrifice. Of course, first he would have to get his other announcements out of the way.

"OK, listen up! You people in the trees, you wanna pay attention? The guys in the bushes, would ya put the woman down? All right. Now, is everybody here? Andy, check the caves. Make sure everybody's out here. And Andy, . . . don't wake up the bears! OK? Remember what happened last time. We can't spare any more people.

"OK, a few things I wanna go over, then I'm gonna tell ya about somethin' new. Somethin' we haven't tried before, so I don't want ya to be nervous. I know ya don't like new things. I remember last year a lotta people freaked out when someone came up with the wheel. People went nuts! They said, Well, this is it, it's all over, it's the end of the world, bla, bla, bla. Then somebody pointed out that we didn't have any axles. I think it was Richie. He said if we really wanted to invent something special, we oughta come up with the axle. I guess you're always gonna have a coupla wise guys.

"But anyway, we went ahead and made a coupla hundred of these big stone wheels, which is kinda stupid when you think about it. The only thing you can do with 'em is roll 'em down the hill. Which isn't such a top notch idea. I think the people who live at the bottom of the hill will bear me out on that.

"OK, movin' along here. It has come to my attention that some people have been drawin' pictures on the walls of the caves. Pictures of bulls, antelopes, a coupla horses. I think I even seen a goat on one wall. Listen, lemme tell you somethin'. It might seem like fun to you, but it looks awful. If ya can't keep the place clean, maybe ya don't deserve a nice cave. Ya don't see the bats drawin' pictures on the walls, do ya? No. They hang upside down, they take a crap, they don't bother anybody.

"You people don't know when you're well off. Maybe ya'd like to go back to livin' in the trees, huh? Remember that? Remember the trees? Competin' with the baboons and gibbons for hazelnuts and loganberries? Degrading! So there'll be no more drawin' on the walls! Coupla thousand years from now, people are gonna come here, and they're gonna study these caves. The last thing they wanna see is a lotta horse pictures on the walls.

"OK, continuin' on. As some of you mighta noticed, last night the fire went out. Coupla the guys on guard duty were jackin' around, playin' grabass, and one of 'em, Octavio, the short guy with the bushy hair. Well, one of the short guys with the bushy hair. Anyways, Octavio fell on the fire, and the fire went out. Unfortunately for Octavio, he died in the incident. Unfortunately for us, he was the only one who knew how to light the fire. So we're gonna have a contest. The first guy to get a fire goin', and keep it goin', wins a prize. It's a hat. Nothin' fancy. Just a regular hat. The kind with the earlaps.

"OK, next item. We're startin' to get some complaints from the women about dating procedures. This mainly concerns the practice of clubbin' the women on the head and draggin' 'em back to the cave by the hair. They would like to discontinue this practice, especially the hair part. It seems some of them go to a lot of trouble and expense to fix up their hair for a date, and they feel the draggin' has a negative effect on their appearance. As far as the clubbin' is concerned, they'd like to elminate that too, because what happens is a lot of 'em have an enjoyable date, and then they can't remember it in the mornin'.

"Movin' right along. As you all know, it's been our practice when we find a new plant that looks good to eat, we test it on the dogs to see if it's poison. Does everyone remember the berries we tested last week on the big brown dog? How many ate the berries simply because the dog didn't die that day? Quite a few. Well, I got bad news. The dog died last night. Apparently it was a slow-actin' poison. Yes, Laszlo? You didn't eat the berries? But this mornin' you ate the dog. Well, Laszlo, ya got about a week. Food chain! How many times do I gotta tell you people? Food chain! By the way, anyone who's gettin' into that new cannibalism crap—I won't mention any names—I'd strongly suggest not eatin' Laszlo—or anyone else for that matter.

"All right, now we gotta talk about the Hated Band of Enemy People Who Live in the Dark Valley. As some of ya might know, they snuck into camp last night and stole a bunch of our stuff. They got those sticks we were savin'. They got the rocks we piled up near the big tree. And they also took sixteen trinkets; the ones we got in a trade with the Friendly Bent-over People from the Tall Mountain Near the Sun. I think it was them. It was either them or the Guys with the Really Big Foreheads Down by the River. Anyways, as I recall, we came off a cool two hundred animal skins for those trinkets, and frankly, the Chief and I think we got screwed. By the way, speakin' of screwin', they also stole several of our women last night. Along with a couple of those sensitive men we've been usin' as women.

"OK, a new problem has come up that we're gonna have to deal with. It concerns the growin' menace of people chewin' the leaves of the dream plant. It's gotten completely outta hand. At first it wasn't so bad. After a long day of huntin', or gatherin'—whatever—people would chew a coupla leaves to relax. Recreational chewin'. No harm, no foul. But then some guys couldn't leave it alone. They would chew way too much and lose control. Some of them became verbally abusive. Of course, they couldn't help what they were sayin'. It wasn't them talkin', it was the leaves. But, hey, nevertheless!

"Then we found out some people were chewin' on the job. Not only endangerin' the lives of their co-hunters or co-gatherers—whatever—but also lowerin' the amount of food we acquire, while somehow, at the same time, greatly increasin' the rate of consumption of their own food. One of the gatherers, a short guy with bushy hair, I think it was Norris, got whacked outta his skull on leaves last week, and he came in from gatherin', with a grand total . . . get this . . . a grand total of six berries and one nut. And this guy had been out in the bushes for eight days!

"But now we're runnin' into an even more serious problem that affects the safety of everyone. It seems that some people are chewin' the leaves and then runnin' around in circles at high speed. As a result we're startin' to get a huge increase in the number of accidents. People are crashin' into each other. Please! Try to remember. Chewin' and runnin' around in circles at high speed don't mix. If you're gonna run around in circles, don't chew; and if you're gonna chew, for God's sake, don't be runnin' around in circles. Designate someone.

"So try to be aware of the signs of leaf abuse. If you're chewin' in the mornin', you got a problem. If you're chewin' alone, you got a problem. It's no disgrace. Get some help. Say no to leaves.

"OK, now, like I said earlier, we got a new thing we're gonna be doin', and I wanna announce it today. It's gonna be a custom. Remember customs? Who can name a custom? Nat? Goin' to sleep at night? Well, that's close, Nat. That's almost like a custom. Who else can name a custom? Killing the animals before we eat them? OK, actually, Jules, that's more like a necessity, isn't it? More like a necessity. Lookin' for a custom. Another custom. Dwayne? Washin' the rocks and dryin' them off before you throw them at the enemy durin' a rock fight? Is that what you been doin', Dwayne? Really! Well, I guess that would explain the disproportionately high number of rock injuries in your squad, wouldn't it?

"Anyway, this new custom is quite different, and it might come as somethin' of a surprise to ya, so make sure you're sittin' down. Or at least leanin' on somethin' firm. You people standin' over near the cliff, you might wanna drift over this way a little.

"Now. I want ya to remember that no matter what I say, this is gonna please the Corn God. OK? [Slowly, as if to children] The new custom . . . is gonna help . . . with the corn. Remember a coupla years ago we had no corn, and we hadda eat the trees? And a lotta people died? How many wanna go back to eatin' the trees? OK, I rest my case. Yeah? Dwayne? You thought the trees were pretty good? Ya never disappoint me, Dwayne, ya know that? Folks, ya don't have to look very far for a tragic example of abusin' the dream plant, do ya?

"All right, here's the new thing we're gonna do, it's called a human sacrifice. Each week, to appease the Corn God, we're gonna kill one member of the tribe. All right, calm down! C'mon, sit down! Hey! Hold on! Hear me out on this, would ya? Just relax and hear me out on this. We're gonna start havin' a human sacrifice every week, probably on Saturday night. That's when everybody seems to loosen up pretty good. So startin' next Saturday night, about the time we run outta berry juice, we're gonna pick one person, probably a young virgin, and we'll throw her in the volcano. All right, girls! Please! Siddown! Please! Stop with the rocks!! Calm down, ladies. We're not gonna do it today. I promise. Relax.

"OK, so we throw the virgin in the volcano. By the way, how many remember the volcano? Remember the fire? Remember the lava? What word comes to mind when we think about the volcano? Hot! Right. The volcano is hot. What's that, Dwayne? No. No way. If this idea's gonna work at all, it's gotta be done while the volcano is actually erupting. I don't think the Corn God is gonna be impressed if we throw some chick in a dormant volcano. It's meaningless. I think he's lookin' for somethin' with a little more screamin' involved.

"OK, so we throw the virgin in the volcano. What's that? How does this help with the corn? Good question. Look, Morley, I just make the announcements, OK? I'm not involved with policy. It came down from the high priests, that's all you gotta know. This is one of those things you just gotta accept on faith. It's like that custom we started last year of cuttin' off a guy's head to keep him from stealin'. At first it seemed severe, am I right? But ya gotta admit, it seems to work.

"OK, one last point: You say, Why does it have to be a young virgin; why can't we throw a wrinkled old man in the volcano? Lemme put it this way. Did y'ever get a real good, close look at the high priests? OK. Once again, I rest my case.

"Now, the only problem we anticipate with this new custom is the distinct possibility of runnin' out of virgins. Ya gotta figure best case scenario we're not gonna see any corn till late next year, so it looks like we're gonna be waxin' virgins at quite a clip. And hey! . . . girls, don't take this the wrong way . . . but we don't have that many virgins to begin with, do we? Ha-ha-ha-ha!! No offense, girls! Really! No, hey, you're very lovely.

"Well, that's it, folks. Thanks for listenin'. Good night. Walk home slowly. And walk safely. In case you didn't notice, the sun went down, and it's completely fuckin' dark."

SOME FAVORITE EUPHEMISMS
(all euphemisms actually observed)

blow job = holistic massage therapy

cheap hotel = limited service lodging

loan-sharking = interim financing

kidnapping = custodial interference

mattress and box spring = sleep system

shack job = live-in companion

truck stop = travel plaza

used videocassette = previously viewed cassette

wife beating = intermittent explosive disorder

theater = performing arts center

manicurist = nail technician

nude beach = clothing optional beach

peephole = observation port

baldness = acquired uncombable hair

body bags = remains pouches

drought = deficit water situation

recession = a meaningful downturn in aggregate output

in love = emotionally involved

room clerk = guest service agent

MORE FAVORITE EUPHEMISMS

uniforms = career apparel

seat belt/air bag = impact management system

prostitute = commercial sex worker

dildo = marital aid

nonbelievers = the unchurched

lying on a job application = résumé enhancement

miscarriage = pregnancy loss

police clubs = batons

smuggling = commodity relocation

porn star = adult entertainer

room service = private dining

nightclub = party space

monkey bars = pipe-frame exercise unit

cardboard box = makeshift home

fingerprinting = digital imaging

fat lady = big woman

junkies = the user population

apartment = dwelling unit

committee = task force

maid = room attendant

salesman = product specialist

EVEN MORE FAVORITE EUPHEMISMS

bad loans = nonperforming assets

seasickness = motion discomfort

gangs = nontraditional organized crime

civilian deaths = collateral damage

gambling joint = gaming resort

mole = beauty mark

garbage collection = environmental services

breast = white meat

thigh = dark meat

sludge = bio-solids

genocide = ethnic cleansing

Jeep = sports utility vehicle

library = learning resources center

junk mail = direct marketing

soda jerk = fountain attendant

soldiers and weapons = military assets

third floor = level three

illegal immigrant = guest worker

Jet ski = personal watercraft

loafers = slip-ons

pOLiTicALly cORRECT LANGUAGE

I know I'm a little late with his, but I'd like to get a few licks in on this bogus topic before it completely disappears from everyone's consciousness.

First, I want to be really clear about one thing: as far as other people's feelings are concerned—especially these "victim groups"—when I deal with them as individuals, I will call them whatever they want. When it's one on one, if some guy wants me to call him a morbidly obese, African-ancestored male with a same-gendered sexual orientation I'll be glad to do that. On the other hand, if he wants me to call him a fat nigger cocksucker, then that's what it will be. I'm here to please.

If I meet a woman who wishes to be referred to as a motion-impaired, same-gender-oriented Italian-American who is difficult to deal with, fine. On the other hand, I am perfectly willing to call her a crippled, Guinea dyke cunt if she prefers. I'm not trying to change anyone's self-image. But! But! When I am speaking generally, and impersonally, about a large group of people, especially these victim groups, I will call them what I think is honest and fair. And I will try not to bullshit myself.

OK, so, who exactly are these victims? Well, first of all, I don't think everyone who says he's a victim automatically qualifies. I don't think a homely, disfigured, bald minority person with a room-temperature IQ who limps and stutters is necessarily always a victim. Although I will say she probably shouldn't be out trying to get work as a receptionist. But maybe that's just the way it oughta be.

I'm more interested in real victims. People who have been chronically and systematically fucked over by the system. Because the United States is a Christian racist nation with a rigged economic system run for three hundred years by the least morally qualified of the two sexes, there were bound to be some real victims. People who've been elaborately fucked over.

The way I see it, this country has only four real victim-groups: Indians, blacks, women, and gays. I purposely left out the Spanish and Asians, because when you look at what happened to the Indians and blacks, the Spanish and Asian people have had a walk in the park. It's not even close. Not to downplay the shit they've had to eat, but in about one hundred years the Spanish and Asians are going to be running this country, so they'll have plenty of chances to get even with the gray people.

Let's get to some of these other non-victims. You probably noticed, elsewhere I used the word fat. I used that word because that's what fat people are. They're fat. They're not large; they're not stout, chunky, hefty, or plump. And they're not big-boned. Dinosaurs are big-boned. These people are not necessarily obese, either. Obese is a medical term. And they're not overweight. Overweight implies there is some correct weight. There is no correct weight. Heavy is also a misleading term. An aircraft carrier is heavy; it's not fat. Only people are fat, and that's what fat people are. They're fat. I offer no apology for this. It is not intended as criticism or insult. It is simply descriptive language. I don't like euphemisms. Euphemisms are a form of lying. Fat people are not gravitationally disadvantaged. They're fat. I prefer seeing things the way they are, not the way some people wish they were.

I don't believe certain groups deserve extra-special names.

For instance, midgets and dwarfs are midgets and dwarfs. They're not little people. Infants are little people; leprechauns are little people. Midgets and dwarfs are midgets and dwarfs. They don't get any taller by calling them little people. I wish their lives were different. I wish they didn't have to walk around staring at other people's crotches, but I can't fix that. And I'm not going to lie about what they are. The politically sensitive language commandos would probably like me to call them "vertically challenged." They're not vertically challenged. A skydiver is vertically challenged. The person who designed the Empire State Building was vertically challenged. Midgets and dwarfs are midgets and dwarfs.

Also, crippled people are crippled, they're not differently-abled. If you insist on using tortured language like differently-abled, then you must include all of us. We're all differently-abled. You can do things I can't do; I can do things you can't do. I can pick my nose with my thumb, and I can switch hands while masturbating and gain a stroke. We're all differently-abled. Crippled people are simply crippled. It's a perfectly honorable word. There is no shame in it. It's in the Bible: "Jesus healed the cripples." He didn't engage in rehabilitative strategies for the physically disadvantaged.

So, leaving aside women and gays for the moment, I've narrowed it down to blacks and Indians. Let's talk about what we ought to call them, and let's talk about what the language commandos would like us to call them. And remember, this has nothing to do with the people themselves. It has to do with the words.

And, by the way, when it comes to these liberal language vandals, I must say I agree with their underlying premise: White Europeans and their descendants are morally unattractive people who are responsible for most of the world's suffering. That part is easy. You would have to be, uh, visually impaired not to see it. The impulse behind political correctness is a good one. But like every good impulse in America it has been grotesquely distorted beyond usefulness.

Clearly, there are victims, but I don't agree that these failed campus revolutionaries know what to do about them. When they're not busy curtailing freedom of speech, they're running around inventing absurd hyphenated names designed to make people feel better. Remember, these are the white elitists in their customary paternalistic role: protecting helpless, inept minority victims. Big Daddy White Boss always knows best.

So, let me tell you how I handle some of these speech issues. First of all, I say "black." I say "black" because most black people prefer "black." I don't say "people of color." People of color sounds like something you see when you're on mushrooms. Besides, the use of people of color is dishonest. It means precisely the same as colored people. If you're not willing to say "colored people," you shouldn't be saying "people of color."

Besides, the whole idea of color is bullshit anyway. What should we call white people? "People of no color"? Isn't pink a color? In fact, white people are not really white at all, they're different shades of pink, olive, and beige. In other words, they're colored. And black people are rarely black. I see mostly different shades of brown and tan. In fact, some light-skinned black people are lighter than the darkest white people. Look how dark the people in India are. They're dark brown, but they're considered white people. What's going on here? May I see the color chart? "People of color" is an awkward, bullshit, liberal-guilt phrase that obscures meaning rather than enhancing it. Shall we call fat people, "people of size"?

By the way, I think the whole reason we're encouraged in this country to think of ourselves as "black and white" (instead of "pink and brown," which is what we are) is that black and white are complete opposites that cannot be reconciled. Black and white can never come together. Pink and brown, on the other hand, might just stand a chance of being blended, might just come together. Can't have that! Doesn't fit the plan.

I also don't say "African-American." I find it completely illogical, and furthermore it's confusing. Which part of Africa are we talking about? What about Egypt? Egypt is in Africa. Egyptians aren't black. They're like the people in India, they're dark brown white people. But they're Africans. So why wouldn't an Egyptian who becomes a U.S. citizen be an African-American?

The same thing goes for the Republic of South Africa. Suppose a white racist from South Africa becomes an American citizen? Well, first of all he'd find plenty of company, but couldn't he also be called an African-American? It seems to me that a racist white South-African guy could come here and call himself African-American just to piss off black people. And, by the way, what about a black person born in South Africa who moves here and becomes a citizen? What is he? An African-South-African-American? Or a South-African-African-American?

All right, back to this hemisphere. How about a black woman who is a citizen of Jamaica? According to P.C. doctrine, she's an African-Jamaican, right? But if she becomes a U.S. citizen, she's a Jamaican-American. And yet if one of these language crusaders saw her on the street, he'd think she was an African-American. Unless he knew her personally in which case he would have to decide between African-Jamaican-American and Jamaican-African-American. Ya know? It's just so much liberal bullshit. Labels divide people. We need fewer labels, not more.

Now, the Indians. I call them Indians because that's what they are. They're Indians. There's nothing wrong with the word Indian. First of all, it's important to know that the word Indian does not derive from Columbus mistakenly believing he had reached "India." India was not even called by that name in 1492; it was known as Hindustan. More likely, the word *Indian* comes from Columbus's description of the people he found here. He was an Italian, and did not speak or write very good Spanish, so in his written accounts he called the Indians, "Una gente in Dios." A people in God. In God. In Dios. Indians. It's a perfectly noble and respectable word.

So let's look at this pussified, trendy bullshit phrase, Native Americans. First of all, they're not natives. They came over the

Bering land bridge from Asia, so they're not natives. There are no natives anywhere in the world. Everyone is from somewhere else. All people are refugees, immigrants, or aliens. If there were natives anywhere, they would be people who still live in the Great Rift valley in Africa where the human species arose. Everyone else is just visiting. So much for the "native" part of Native American.

As far as calling them "Americans" is concerned, do I even have to point out what an insult this is? Jesus Holy Shit Christ! We steal their hemisphere, kill twenty or so million* of them, destroy five hundred separate cultures, herd the survivors onto the worst land we can find, and now we want to name them after ourselves? It's appalling. Haven't we done enough damage? Do we have to further degrade them by tagging them with the repulsive name of their conquerers?

And as far as these classroom liberals who insist on saying "Native American" are concerned, here's something they should be told: It's not up to you to name people and tell them what they ought to be called. If you'd leave the classroom once in a while, you'd find that most Indians are insulted by the term Native American. The American Indian Movement will tell you that if you ask them.

The phrase "Native American" was invented by the U.S. government Department of the Interior in 1970. It is an inventory term used to keep track of people. It includes Hawaiians, Eskimos, Samoans, Micronesians, Polynesians, and Aleuts. Anyone who uses the phrase *Native American*

---

* Before 1492 there were 25 million people in Central America. By 1579 there were 2 million.

is assisting the U.S. government in its effort to obliterate people's true identities.

Do you want to know what the Indians would like to be called? Their real names: Adirondack, Delaware, Massachuset, Narraganset, Potomac, Illinois, Miami, Alabama, Ottawa, Waco, Wichita, Mohave, Shasta, Yuma, Erie, Huron, Susquehanna, Natchez, Mobile, Yakima, Wallawalla, Muskogee, Spokan, Iowa, Missouri, Omaha, Kansa, Biloxi, Dakota, Hatteras, Klamath, Caddo, Tillamook, Washoe, Cayuga, Oneida, Onondaga, Seneca, Laguna, Santa Ana, Winnebago, Pecos, Cheyenne, Menominee, Yankton, Apalachee, Chinook, Catawba, Santa Clara, Taos, Arapaho, Blackfoot, Blackfeet, Chippewa, Cree, Cheyenne, Mohawk, Tuscarora, Cherokee, Seminole, Choctaw, Chickasaw, Comanche, Shoshone, Two Kettle, Sans Arc, Chiricahua, Kiowa, Mescalero, Navajo, Nez Perce, Potawatomi, Shawnee, Pawnee, Chickahominy, Flathead, Santee, Assiniboin, Oglala, Miniconjou, Osage, Crow, Brulé, Hunkpapa, Pima, Zuni, Hopi, Paiute, Creek, Kickapoo, Ojibwa, Shinnicock.

You know, you'd think it would be a fairly simple thing to come over to this continent, commit genocide, eliminate the forests, dam up the rivers, build our malls and massage parlors, sell our blenders and whoopee cushions, poison ourselves with chemicals, and let it go at that. But no. We have to compound the insult. Native Americans! I'm glad the Indians have gambling casinos now. It makes me happy that dimwitted white people are losing their rent money to the Indians. Maybe the Indians will get lucky and win their country back. Probably they wouldn't want it. Look what we did to it.

MISFORTUNE

People like to say that no matter how bad off your life is, there is always someone worse off than you. I guess it's a source of comfort. It's nice to know that while they're removing a bone from your throat, the man in the next room has a four hundred-pound tumor in his groin.

But the idea that there is always someone worse off leads to the logical conclusion that somewhere in the world there is a person who is in worse shape than everybody else. Some guy who has almost six billion people doing better than he is.

But, in reality, as you get down to the bottom of the bad-shape pile, it becomes harder and harder to know who's doing worse. Is a blind, paralyzed, maniac really better off than a three-foot, paraplegic imbecile? Tough call.

Then there's always my "Plus-a-Headache" formula. No matter how horrible and painful a person's condition may be, it can always be made worse by simply adding a headache: "He was poor, ignorant, diseased, lonely, depressed, and abandoned—plus he had a headache."

Look on the bright side: The headache will very likely go away.

THE GRIEF/TRAGEDY/SYMPATHY INDUSTRY

Everyone complains about this being a "victim society." Well, I don't know about the victim society, but I would like to talk about the "Grief, Tragedy, and Sympathy Industry."

The news media are playing a game with you. You're being fed a large ration of other people's troubles designed to keep your mind off the things that should really be bothering you. I guess the media figure if you're sitting around feeling sorry for every sick, injured, or dead person they can scrounge up, you'll have less time to dwell on how fucked up your own life is, and what bad shape this culture is really in.

I'm not so much opposed to grief per se, as I am to public media grief. My attitude is fuck sick people and fuck a dead person. Unless I knew them. And, if so, I'll handle it on my own, thank you. I don't need media guidance to experience sorrow.

Above all, I object to the abuse of the word *tragedy*. Every time some asshole stops breathing these days it's called a tragedy. The word has been devalued. You can't call every death a tragedy and expect the word to mean anything. For instance, multiple deaths do not automatically qualify as tragedies. Just because a man kills his wife and three kids, her lover, his lover, the baby-sitter, the mailman, the Amway lady, and the guy from Publishers' Clearing House and then blows his own brains out doesn't mean a tragedy has occurred. It's interesting. It's entertaining to read about. But it's not a tragedy.

The death of a child is also not automatically a tragedy. Some guy backing over his kid in the driveway is not a tragedy, it's a bad, bad mistake. A tragedy is a literary work in which the main character comes to ruin as a consequence of a moral weakness or a fatal flaw. Shakespeare wrote tragedies. A family of nine being wiped out when a train hits their camper is not a tragedy. It's called a traffic accident.

You wanna know what a tragedy is? A tragedy is when you see some fat bastard in the airport with pockmarks on his face and his belly hanging out, and he's with a woman who has bad teeth and multiple bruises, and that night he's gonna make her suck his dick. That's a tragedy. They don't mention that a lot on TV.

The media often refer to the killing of a white policeman as a *tragedy*. Why is that more tragic than the same white policeman killing an unarmed black kid? Why is it never a tragedy on TV when a white cop kills a black kid? It's never presented in that way. The whites save *tragedy* for themselves. Why is that?

The media have elevated the marketing of bathos and sympathy to a fine art. But I gotta tell ya, I really don't care about a paraplegic who climbs a mountain and then skis cross-country for 50 miles; I'm not interested in a one-legged veteran who ice skates across Canada to raise money for children's prosthetics. I have no room for some guy without a nervous system who becomes the state wrestling champion; or a man who loses his torso in Vietnam and later holds his breath for six months to promote spina bifida research; or someone born with no heart who lives to be ninety-five and helps everyone in his neighborhood neaten up their lawns.

Is this all we can find in America that passes for personal drama? People overcoming long odds? God, it's so boring and predictable.

And does this mean we are supposed to admire people simply because of the order of their luck? Because their bad luck came first? What about the reverse? What about people who start well and then fail spectacularly in life? People who were born with every privilege and given every possible gift and talent, who had all the money they needed, were surrounded by good people, and then went out and fucked their lives up anyway? Isn't that drama too? Isn't that equally ineresting? In fact, I find it more interesting. More like true tragedy.

I'd prefer to hear something like that once in a while, rather than this pseudo-inspirational bullshit that the media feel they have to feed us in order to keep our minds off America's decline. If they're going to insist that we really need to know about sick babies and cripples who tap dance and quadraplegic softball players, why don't they simply have a special television program called "Inspirational Stories"? That way I can turn the fuckin' thing off. I'm tired of people battling the odds. Fuck the odds. And fuck the people who battle them.

After a while don't you just get weary of being told that some kid in Minnesota needs a new liver? Kids didn't need new livers when I was growing up. We had good livers. What are they feeding these kids that suddenly they all need new livers? I think it's the gene pool. Nature used to eliminate the weak, imperfect kids before they were old enough to reproduce their flaws. Now we have a medical industry dedicated to keeping people alive just long enough to pass along their bad genes to another generation. It's medical arrogance, and it works against nature's plan. I'm sick of hearing about a baby being kept alive on a resuscitator while doctors wait for a kidney to be flown in on a private jet contributed by some corporation seeking good publicity because they just killed six thousand people in Pakistan with a chemical spill. I'm tired of this shit being presented in the context of real news. Prurient gossip about sick people is not real news. It's emotional pandering.

The real news is that there are millions upon millions of sick babies and cripples and addicts and criminals and misfits and diseased and mentally ill and hungry people who need help. Not to mention all the middle-class normals who swear things are just fine but spend three hours a day commuting, and whose dull, meaningless lives are being stolen from them by soulless corporations. But the media don't bother with all that. They like to simply cover their designated Victims of the Week, so they can see themselves as somehow noble. They highlight certain cases, making them appear exceptional. And when they do, they admit they are simply unable and unwilling to report the totality of the Great American Social Nightmare.

DEATH IS ALMOST FUN THESE DAYS

Seems to me it wasn't long ago that when an OLD PERSON DIED the UNDERTAKER put him in a COFFIN, and you sent FLOWERS to the FUNERAL HOME where the MORTICIAN held the WAKE. Then, after the FUNERAL, they put him in a HEARSE and DROVE him to the CEMETERY, where they BURIED his BODY in a GRAVE.

Now when a SENIOR CITIZEN PASSES AWAY, he is placed in a BURIAL CONTAINER, and you send FLORAL TRIBUTES to the SLUMBER ROOM where the GRIEF THERAPIST supervises the VIEWING. After the MEMORIAL SERVICE, the FUNERAL COACH TRANSPORTS THE DEPARTED to the GARDEN OF REMEMBRANCE, where his EARTHLY REMAINS are INTERRED in their FINAL RESTING PLACE.

R.I.P. ON THE VCR

You know where you never see a camcorder? At a funeral. Wouldn't that be fun? Especially if you didn't know any of the people there. Why not go to a stranger's funeral, and bring your camcorder? Have a little fun! Zoom in on the corpse's nose hairs. Then pull back, and pan over to the widow's tears. Get a tight shot of that. Do a montage of people wracked with grief. Then go home and put a laugh track on it! Smoke a joint and show it to your friends. That would be a lot of fun.

LEGAL MURDER ONCE A MONTH

You can talk about capital punishment all you want, but I don't think you can leave everything up to the government. Citizens should be willing to take personal responsibility. Every now and then you've got to do the right thing, and go out and kill someone on your own. I believe the killing of human beings is just one more function of government that needs to be privatized.

I say this because I believe most people know at least one other person they wish were dead. One other person whose death would make their life a little easier. A sexual rival; an abuser; a tormentor at school; a parent who's been draining the family nest egg by lingering too long on life support. It's a natural, human instinct. In fact, in the psychological literature it's technically referred to as, "Jesus, I wish that son of a bitch was dead!" Don't run from it. Society must find a way to accommodate this very understandable human instinct.

173

And so, I offer a plan: Legal Murder Once a Month. Under this plan, every thirty days each person in America will be allowed to kill one other person without incurring punishment. One murder per person, per month. But you can't kill just anybody. It's not random. Each month there will be a different type of person it's OK to kill. For instance, one month it would be all right to kill a business associate. (For you blue-collar guys, that means someone at work.) That month, kill anybody at work—no punishment. But you must have a good reason; none of this weak shit, "I caught him fucking my wife." It has to be a good reason. Like, "The guy is just a real asshole."

Another month we would have a day when it's OK to kill a relative. Actually, you might want two days for this, one for in-laws, and one for blood relatives. In fact, you might even need a week. Seven days, seven dead relatives. A festival! The Seven Dead Relatives Festival. Christmas week! There's a good time for family resentment. Lots of old, festering patho-logical flotsam bobbing to the surface like buoyant turds. Christmas! Peace on Earth and a nice stack of dead relatives under the tree. And forgive what may seem a tacky note, but this plan might also help simplify your Xmas shopping.

All right, what about spouses? You gotta have a day for killing spouses, although I don't think you'd want to do this one too often. You know how some guys are, they'd be goin' through ten or twelve old ladies a year. No, this one should be an annual event with a one-spouse limit. In fact, why not just have an annual spouse-hunting season? You must get a license, you must wear bright orange, and you must be accompanied by three drunken friends. And please take note, those of you who aren't married and are merely living together will not be allowed to kill each other until you have taken your sacred vows.

All right, we've covered relatives and spouses. Now, how about that certain someone else? Someone who really deserves to die? The ex-spouse! The exes of both sexes. The ex-husband, usually referred to in court documents as "the asshole." And, of course, that other towering archetypal figure in divorce law, "the cunt"!

In fact, I think we ought to just combine spouses and ex-spouses and stretch this one into a full week as well. Do I smell another holiday festival here? Is this possibly Easter week we're talkin' about? I think so! And I'm gonna give you a special deal. Not only will you be allowed to kill your ex-spouse, but you'll also get to kill their lawyer. It's a two-for-one, Easter Bunny, Resurrection special. One man rises from the dead, two people take his place. By the way, are you beginning to sense that perhaps there's a place for the Disney corporation in all of this? Just a thought.

And while we're at it, why don't we honor Freud by having a day for killing parents? This is something that doesn't happen nearly often enough as far as I'm concerned. Why should the Menendez Brothers have all the fun? Get into that living room, whip out the shotgun, and launch your parents into the great beyond so they can be with their loving God. Do the folks a favor. What kind of an ungrateful child are you? By the way, if you're wondering why parents aren't already covered in the Seven Dead Relatives

Festival, it's because parents are special people, and they deserve special treatment.

Here would be another handy event: Kill-a-Neighbor-Day. A perfect way to settle old scores and perhaps, at the same time, upgrade the neighborhood. And just to provide you a little flexibility, for our purposes a neighbor will be considered anyone who lives in your zip code.

You know, now that I think of it, it would probably make sense to simply have Wild-Card Day. One day a year when everyone can just go out and kill whomever the fuck they want. Many of us have long lists of specific, worthy targets who don't fall into any of the established categories. Retail clerks, landlords, teachers, salesmen, telephone solicitors; the asshole Connecticut people in the blue Volvo station wagon; the arrogant yuppie prick at the laundromat who acted so superior about his natural fibers; and how about that snotty blonde bitch on the "Six O'Clock News"? The one who keeps braying, "Thank God, no one was hurt," every time someone so much as backs into a lamppost.

Now, let me quickly point out that my Legal Murder Once a Month plan has three strict rules: First, it isn't cumulative. You can't save up all your murders for a year and then go waltzing into McDonald's and spoil everyone's Egg McMuffin. You get one murder a month, that's it. Use it or lose it.

Rule number two: You can't hire someone to do the killing for you. You have to do it yourself. And if you're squeamish, take my word for it, you'll get over that. There's nothing to it. I, myself, have killed six people. All random, all undetected, no way to trace them to me. And, let me tell you, there's nothin' like it. It's a great feeling. Yeah, I know, you're thinking. "Aw, he's a comedian. He's just sayin' that stuff." Good. That's exactly what I want you to think.

Rule number three: You can never kill your own offspring. It's just off-limits. OK? No killing your own children. Of course, if they really deserve it; if they're really bad news, they'll probably piss someone else off, and that person will take care of the job for you.

And all you civic-minded dipshits, I want you to know there's nothing in the constitution to prevent any of this. The state doesn't actually oppose murder, it simply objects to those who go into business for themselves. When it comes to the taking of human life, the federal government doesn't want free-lance competition.

Life is cheap, never forget it. Corporations make marketing decisions by weighing the cost of being sued for your death against the cost of making the product safer. Your life is a factor in cost-effectiveness. So when you talk about murder, don't confine your discussion to individuals.

Besides, there's nothing wrong with murder in the first place. Murder is a part of life. My society taught me that. And my species is really good at it. I belong to the only species in the history of the world that systematically tortures and murders its own members for pleasure, profit, and convenience.

See how easily we figured all that out? How easy that was? People think life is real complicated. Actually, there's nothing to it. Once you leave out all the bullshit they teach you in school, life gets really simple.

FUN FOES

Since I hold no real national allegiances, when it comes to armed conflict around the world I tend to root for the side that will provide me with the most entertainment. Saddam Hussein is a case in point. Any head of state who says, "We will walk on your corpses and crush your skulls, and you will swim in your own blood," is my kinda guy. You just don't hear that kind of shit anymore. This man obviously has great potential to provide me with amusing diversion.

In fact, all these Middle-East religious fanatics are brimming with entertainment potential. On CNN I recently saw video of 200 Islamic student-suicide bombers who were graduating from suicide-bomber school. They were singing what was apparently the school fight song: "Our blessings to you who fight at the gates of the enemy and knock on heaven's door with his skulls in your hands." How can Christians and Jews ever hope to compete with these folks who obviously enjoy their work so much?

LET'S ALL KILL EACH OTHER ACCORDING TO THE RULES

I don't understand the Geneva Convention and the whole idea of having rules for fighting a war. Why? Is it really more than just a way of reassuring ourselves we're all quite civilized, as we pour our hearts and minds and fortunes into mass killing? It seems to me like hypocritical bullshit. If the object is to win, wars should be fought with no holds barred; otherwise, why bother suiting up? As it is now, a winner is declared, and yet the issue has not been settled by all possible means.

Additionally, if the object is to kill the enemy, why treat their wounded? Treating their wounded requires resources taken from your own effort to achieve victory. Does this make sense if you're trying to win? Oh, yeah. Civilized.

My doubts about having rules for combat likewise extend to street fighting. I've heard guys whine about someone throwing a "sucker punch." Are they kidding? A guy wants to reduce your ass to a small bloody pile, and you're going to warn him before hitting him? Get fucking lucid! And lose all that dopey shit about fair play. It's out of place if the object is to win. (Is it?)

Also, as far as kicking someone when he's down is concerned, what is the problem here? Again, the object is to win, yes? Well, if he gets up, you might lose; therefore he must not get up. He needs to be kicked. You said you wanted to win. Or are you people just fucking around? I suspect that might be the case. Well, stop fucking around and make up your mind. You're telling me a man will fuck another man's wife, drive him out of business, cut him off and nearly kill him in traffic, but he shouldn't sneak punch, or kick him when he's down? I don't get it.

Another thing I don't understand is the objection to so-called dirty play in sports such as football. These are big, tough guys who are desperate to prove how manly they are; that they're not soft. That's why they play these games in the first place. Well, why not let them play "dirty" and let's find out how tough they really are?

It's been shown that small, dedicated groups of men can easily find ways of policing and disciplining those among them who cross the line. It's called vigilantism, and it's very efficient. Please don't tell a bunch of six-foot-six, three hundred-pounders in helmets and pads they can't spear and punch and put their thumbs in each other's eyes.

You'll miss all the fun. And you'll be keeping them from pursuing their calling at its highest level.

I also don't understand terrorists who call the police to warn them about a bomb. Do I need even explain my dismay at this one?

You know, folks, if this old world had any imagination, wars would be fought without codes and conventions, alley fighting would be standard, and the only rules in sports would govern the uniforms. Then we'd have some real fun.

But I fear that doesn't suit you, and so I return to the notion that produced these thoughts in the first place: You people shouldn't be fighting at all.

UNKNOWN SOLDIER

I recently visited an interesting site in Washington, D.C. You've heard of the Tomb of the Unknown Soldier? This is the Tomb of the *Well*-Known Soldier. No one knows about it. Isn't that odd? Everyone knows about the Unknown Soldier, but no one knows about the Well-Known Soldier. Makes you think, doesn't it? Maybe not.

They're also planning the Tomb of the Well-Known-but-Widely-Disliked Soldier. And then they're gonna build the Tomb of the Well-Liked-but-Poorly-Understood Soldier.

One other interesting fact before we leave this subject. I assume you know that Britain, France, and Canada all have Unknown Soldiers of their own. Well, oddly enough, all three of those soldiers knew each other. Kinda makes the hair on the back of your neck stand up, doesn't it? Maybe not.

IF ONLY WE WERE HUMAN

This species is a dear, hateful, sweet, barbaric, tender, vile, intelligent, confused, virtuous, evil, thoughtful, perverted, generous, greedy species. In short, great entertainment.

As I said before, humans are the only species that systematically tortures and murders its own for pleasure and personal gain. In fact, we are the only species that systematically tortures and murders its own, period.

We are serial killers. All our poems and symphonies and oils on canvas will never change that. Man's noble aspect is the aberration.

Those who argue that art and philosophy are proof of human worth neglect to mention that, in the scheme we have devised, artists and philosophers are completely powerless and largely without prestige. Art, music, and philosophy are merely poignant examples of what we might have been had not the priests and traders gotten hold of us.

Most animals, when fighting one of their own, will show aggressive behavior, but very little hostility or intention to harm. And when the outcome of the struggle is inevitable, the losing animal will signal its defeat by exposing its most vulnerable part to the victor, affording it the opportunity to finish the kill. The victor then walks away without inflicting further harm. These are the creatures we feel superior to.

LOCK AND LOAD

The rate of U.S. Marine suicides has been rising in recent years. The biggest jump came at a time when the Marine Corps was being reduced in size, and so, many of these men were barred from reenlisting. I guess they realized that the odds against death had suddenly improved, and they might actually have to face life. So they killed themselves. Strange, huh? I like that sort of thing. It's entertaining.

PEACE ON YOU

I'm not disturbed by war. More like entertained. War may be a lot of things, but it's never a bad show. It's the original Greatest Show on Earth. Otherwise, why would they call it a "theater of war"? I love it. And as far as I'm concerned, the show must go on.

But I realize there are some people who really worry about this kind of thing, and so, as a good citizen, I offer two ideas for peace. It's the least I can do.

Many people work on war plans; not too many work on peace plans. They even have a war college at Ft. McNair, Washington. They call it the National Defense University, but it's a war college. They don't have a peace college.

And they have war plans for every contingency, no matter how remote. If Easter Island gives us some crap tomorrow, we have a plan in a computer that tells us exactly how to thoroughly bomb the shit out of Easter Island. You name the country, we've got the plan. Chad, Myanmar, Upper Volta, Burkina Faso, Liechtenstein. Just give us some crap, and we'll come there, and bomb the shit out of you! 'Cause we've got a plan.

Well, so do I. Two of them. George's plans for peace:

My first plan is worldwide, year-round, nonstop folk dancing. In short, everyone in the world would be required to dance all the time. It leaves very little time for fighting, and what combat does occur is inefficient, because the combatants are constantly in motion.

When it was suggested that this plan might be impractical, I offered an alternative wherein only half the people would be dancing at any given time. The problem with this was the distinct possibility that while half the people were dancing, the other half would be robbing their homes.

So now I've stripped it down to a symbolic plan: twenty-four-hour, nonstop, worldwide folk dancing, once a year. Each year, on a designated day, everyone in the world would stop what they were doing and dance for twenty-four-hours.

Any kind of dancing you want. Square dance, minuet, grind, peabody, cakewalk, mazurka, samba, mashed potato. Doesn't matter. Just get out there and dance. Even hospital patients, shut-ins, cripples, and people on life support; if you're too sick to dance, you just die. While the doctors and nurses keep dancing. This would be a good way to weed out the weaker people. Dance or die! Natural selection with a beat.

One good result, of course, would be that during the actual dancing, no fighting could take place. But the plan would also tend to reduce violence during the remainder of the year, because for six months following the dance, everyone would be talking about how much fun they had had, and for the six months after that, they would all be busy planning what to wear to next year's dance.

Another plan I have is World Peace Through Formal Introductions. The idea is that everyone in the world would be required to meet everyone else in the world, formally, at least once. You'd have to look the person in the eye, shake hands, repeat their name, and try to remember one outstanding physical characteristic. My theory is, if you knew everyone in the world personally, you'd be less inclined to fight them in a war: "Who? The Malaysians? Are you kidding? I know those people!"

The biggest problem with compulsory, world-wide formal introductions would be logistics. How would it work? Would you line up everyone in the world single file and have one person at a time move down the line meeting all the others? And then when they finish they get on the end of the line, and the next person starts?

Or would you divide everyone into two long lines and have them move past each other laterally? That seems inefficient, because, for at least part of the time, each line would have a large number of people with nothing to do. And also, once you finished the first pass, everyone would still have to meet the people in their own line.

Either way, it would take a very long time. In fact, children would be born during the introductions, and then you'd have to meet them, too.

And it's probably important to remember that because of their longer names, some nationalities would move through the line more slowly than others. Russians, for example. Russian names tend to be long. If you ever bought an ID bracelet for a Russian person, you know what I mean. The engraving alone can run over two hundred dollars.

I'm afraid the Russians would move through the line very slowly: "Vladimir Denisovitch Zhirinovski, this is Yevgeny Vasily Arbatov. Yevgeny Vasily Arbatov, meet Vladimir Denisovitch Zhirinovski." Major delay.

On the other hand, the Chinese tend to have short names. "Chin Lu, Wu Han. Wu Han, Chin Lu." Bing! See ya later! Movin' right along. Which is why there are so many Chinese: less time saying hello, more time to fuck.

Peace on you. But only if you really deserve it.

COME BACK AND SEE US, HEAR?

I suppose it would be nice if reincarnation were a reality, but I have problems with the math. At some point, originally, there must have been a time when there were only two human beings. They both died, and presumably their souls were reincarnated into two other bodies. But that still leaves us with only two souls. We now have nearly six billion people on the planet. Where are all the extra souls coming from? Is someone printing up souls? Wouldn't that tend to lower their value?

SHORT TAKES (Part 2)

I only respect horoscopes that are specific: "Today, Neil Perleman, wearing tight-fitting wool knickers, will kill you on the crosstown bus."

Sometimes we dismiss something by substituting the letters "s-h-m" for the initial consonant sound in the word and then repeating the word itself: "Taxes, shmaxes!" But suppose the thing you're dismissing already starts with the "s-h-m" sound? For instance, how do you dismiss a person named Schmidt?

When a ghostwriter dies, how many people come back?

I'm in favor of personal growth as long as it doesn't include malignant tumors.

Whenever I hear about a "peace-keeping force," I wonder, If they're so interested in peace, why do they use force?

The bigger they are, the worse they smell.

SATAN IS
COOL

Once, at a school function, I received a dressing down for not dressing up.

The keys to America: the cross, the brew, the dollar, and the gun.

My watch stopped. I think I'm down a quartz.

A meltdown sounds like fun. Like some kind of cheese sandwich.

Sex always has consequences. When Hitler's mother spread her legs that night, she effectively canceled out the spreading of fifteen to twenty million other pairs of legs.

A parawhore is a woman who keeps you aroused until they can get you to a real whore.

No one can ever know for sure what a deserted area looks like.

Why don't they put child molesters in a fondling home?

The difference between show business and a gang bang is that in show business everybody wants to go on last.

Don Ho can sign autographs 3.4 times faster than Efrem Zimbalist Jr.

The truth is, Pavlov's dog trained Pavlov to ring his bell just before the dog salivated.

A scary dream makes your heart beat faster. Why doesn't the part of your brain that controls your heartbeat realize that another part of your brain is making the whole thing up? Don't these people communicate?

I never watch "Sesame Street"; I know most of that stuff.

I read that somewhere out west recently a National Wilderness Area was closed for two days because it was too windy.

 e are conditioned to notice and emphasize the differences among ourselves, instead of the similarities. The corporate-style partitioning begins early in life: fetus, newborn, infant, toddler, preschool, lower school, middle school, junior high, senior high, pre-teen, teen. Get in your box and stay there!

THE STATUS QUO ALWAYS SUCKS

Is the kidney a bean-shaped organ, or is the bean a kidney-shaped legume?

I like Florida; everything is in the eighties. The temperatures, the ages, and the IQs.

When you cut the legs off jeans to make cutoffs, don't you feel foolish for just a moment as you stand there holding two useless denim legs?

Why does *Filipino* start with an *F* and *Philippines* start with *Ph*?

I think in retaliation the Jews should be allowed to kill six million Germans. It's only fair. With fifty years of compound interest. That would come to about 110 million Germans. That oughta put a nice dent in bratwurst consumption.

I heard about some guy called the Marrying Rapist. He operates with a minister-partner who performs a wedding ceremony just before the rape. Police are looking for two men in tuxedos and sneakers. Possibly carrying rice.

think tobacco and alcohol warnings are too general. They should be more to the point: "People who smoke will eventually cough up small brown pieces of lung." And "Warning! Alcohol will turn you into the same asshole your father was."

A fast car that passes you at night is going somewhere.

I recently had a ringing in my ear. The doctors looked inside and found a small bell.

IF IT AIN'T BROKE, BREAK IT

If Frank Sinatra owed you a favor, it would be fun to ask him to have one of his buddies kill Andy Williams.

I get a nice safe feeling when I see a police car, and I realize I'm not driving around with a trunkful of cocaine.

I'm offering a special prize for first Buick on the moon.

Why do shoelaces only come in certain sizes?

the public will never become concerned about global warming or the greenhouse effect. These words just aren't scary enough. Global means all-encompassing, warming connotes comfort, green equals growth, and house equals shelter. Growth, shelter, and all-encompassing comfort. Doesn't sound like much of a threat. Relax.

How can a color be artificial? I look at red Jell-O, and it's just as red as it can be.

Why is it the other side of the street always crosses the street when I do?

In Rome, the emperor sat in a special part of the Coliseum known as the Caesarian section.

Sometimes, when I'm told to use my own discretion, if no one is looking I'll use someone else's. But I always put it back.

BOTHER THE WEAK

I don't see the problem with devil worship.

You know what type of cosmetic surgery you never hear about? Nose enlargement.

My phone number is seventeen. We got one of the early ones.

What goes through a bird's mind when he finds himself flying through a fireworks display?

If you nail a tool shed closed, how do you put the hammer away?

Why are there no recreational drugs taken in suppository form?

When I'm working, and the television is on, I always tune in a program I like. If I'm going to ignore something, I want it to be something I enjoy.

No one is ever completely alone; when all is said and done, you always have yourself.

I admire an intelligent man with really unattractive, badly stained and crooked teeth who makes a lot of money and still doesn't get his teeth fixed. It's an interesting choice.

Imagine meeting your maker and finding out it's Frito-Lay.

have you ever groped blindly through the middle of a packed suitcase trying to find something and then suddenly realized with horror that the razor blades had come unwrapped?

I was taken to the hospital for observation. I stayed several days, didn't observe anything, and left.

A tree: First you chop it down, then you chop it up.

I'd hate to be an alcoholic with Alzheimer's. Imagine needing a drink and forgetting where you put it.

Whenever I see a huge crowd, I always wonder how many of the people have hazelnuts in their intestines.

Sometimes I can't recall my mental blocks, so I try not to think about it.

did you ever notice how important the last bite of a candy bar is? All the while you're eating it, you're aware that you have less and less remaining. Then, as you get to the end, if something happens to that last piece, you feel really cheated.

WOOD KILLS

If a cigarette smoker wakes up from a seven-year coma, does he want a cigarette?

There is a small town out west where the entire population is made up of the full-grown imaginary childhood friends of present-day adults.

If a painting can be forged well enough to fool experts, why is the original so valuable?

Valentine's Day is devoted to love. Why don't we have a day devoted to hatred? The raw, visceral hatred that is felt every hour of the day by ordinary people, but is repressed for reasons of social order. I think it would be very cathartic, and it would certainly make for an exciting six o'clock news.

I'm very lucky. The only time I was ever up shit creek, I just happened to have a paddle with me.

the Japanese culture is very big on martial arts and spiritual disciplines. So when a guy tells me he is studying something that has a Japanese name, I know he has either embarked on a mystical journey or is learning how to break someone's neck with two fingers.

Baseball is the only major sport that appears backwards in a mirror.

WHO STOLE THE BANANA GUACAMOLE?

Virginia has passed a law limiting people to the purchase of one gun per person per month. But if you can show the need for more than one gun a month, you can apply to the police for an exemption. "Listen, officer, we've got a really dysfunctional family here, and . . ."

Why does it always take longer to go somewhere than it does to come back?

People tell you to have a safe trip, as if you have some control over it.

Conservatives say if you don't give the rich more money, they will lose their incentive to invest. As for the poor, they tell us they've lost all incentive because we've given them too much money.

Why is the hot water on the left? I think it's so you can use your right hand to test how hot it is.

People love to admit they have bad handwriting or that they can't do math. And they will readily admit to being awkward: "I'm such a klutz!" But they will never admit to having a poor sense of humor or being a bad driver.

Have you ever noticed that the lawyer smiles more than the client?

E-I-E-I-O is actually a gross misspelling of the word *farm*.

If you can't beat them, arrange to have them beaten.

A recent story in the media said that some firemen in Chicago had refused to enter a burning building because it was too hot.

KILL YOUR PET

No one ever mentions when the swallows leave Capistrano. Do they die there?

The lazy composer still had several scores to settle.

At what point in his journey does an emigrant become an immigrant?

In a factory that makes bathroom disinfectant, the whole factory smells like the bathroom.

We have mileage, yardage, and footage, why don't we have inchage?

Travel tip: Economy-section farts on an inbound flight from the Third World are the deadliest a traveler will ever encounter.

Every time you use the phrase *all my life* it has a different meaning.

Great scientific discoveries: jiggling the toilet handle.

When will the rhetorical questions all end?

Why do they call it a garbage disposal? The stuff isn't garbage until after you dispose of it.

A cemetery is a place where dead people live.

Do the people who hate blacks but think they're really good dancers ever stop to think how much better blacks would dance if fewer people hated them?

I do something about the weather. I stay home.

"Let's stop underage drinking before it starts." Please explain this to me. It sounds tricky.

When I'm really bored, I sit home and translate the writing on foreign biscuits.

Political discourse has been reduced to "Where's the beef?" "Read my lips," and "Make my day." Where are the assassins when we really need them?

GANDHI ATE MILK DUDS

Hard work is for people short on talent.

Alter and change are supposed to be synonyms, but altering your trousers and changing your trousers are quite different things.

My back hurts; I think I over-schlepped.

The news story said someone had overcome a fatal disease. Wow!

A Bible makes a delicious meal. Simply rub with olive oil and minced garlic, and bake one hour in a 375-degree oven. Serve with oven-roasted potatoes and a small tossed salad. Serves two. Dee-leesh!

Recently, in a public bathroom, I used the handicapped stall. As I emerged, a man in a wheelchair asked me indignantly, "Are you handicapped?" Gathering all my aplomb, I looked him in the eye and said, "Not now. But I was before I went in there."

Threatening postcard: "Wish you were here, but if you come here I will kill you!"

I wanted to be a Boy Scout, but I had all the wrong traits. They were looking for kids who were trustworthy, loyal, helpful, friendly, courteous, kind, obedient, cheerful, thrifty, brave, clean, and reverent. Whereas I tended to be devious, fickle, obstructive, hostile, impolite, mean, defiant, glum, extravagant, cowardly, dirty, and sacrilegious.

How is it possible to be seated on a standing committee?

195

I have come up with a single sentence that includes all of the seven deadly sins: greed, anger, pride, lust, gluttony, sloth, and envy. Here it is. "It enrages me that I, a clearly superior person, should have less money than my neighbor, whose wife I would love to fuck if I weren't so busy eating pork chops and sleeping all day."

Recent polls reveal that some people have never been polled. Until recently.

did you ever run over somebody with your car? And then you panic? So you back up and run over them again? Did you notice the second crunch was not quite as loud?

If I had just one wish it would be to write the letter z better in longhand.

have you noticed, whenever there's a problem in this country they get a bunch of celebrities or children together to sing a song about it? Drought, famine, drugs; they sing a song about it. This is an idea that grew out of the '60s peace movement. The idea then was that if enough "good" people sang, chanted, and held hands, all the "evil" people would give up their money, weapons, and power. Worked great, didn't it?

WE ARE ALL PRECANCEROUS

I read about a woman who had sixty-three distinct personalities. Jesus! It would take long enough just finding out how everyone was feeling in the morning, can you imagine trying to plan a vacation?

I put a dollar in one of those change machines. Nothing changed.

After the year 2000, I hope the crime of the century happens real soon, so I get to read about it.

They say if you outlaw guns, only outlaws and criminals will have guns. Well, shit, those are precisely the people who need them.

I once found a throw rug in a catch basin.

One time, a few years ago, Oprah had a show about women who fake orgasms. Not to be outdone, Geraldo came right back with a show about men who fake bowel movements.

It is now possible for a child to have five parents: sperm donor, egg donor, the surrogate mother who carries the fetus, and two adoptive parents. It renders the statement "He has his mother's eyes" rather meaningless.

The new, modern Swiss Army knife has an ear-piercing tool and a roach clip.

One of the best expressions in the English language is, "Who says so?" I guarantee, if you keep saying, "Who says so?" long enough, sooner or later someone will take you into custody.

It's hard for me to believe that the small amount of water I take from the water cooler can produce such a large bubble.

Infant crib death is caused by grandparents' breath.

've always wanted to place a personal ad no one would answer: "Elderly, depressed, accident-prone junkie, likes Canadian food and Welsh music, seeking rich, well-built, oversexed, female deaf mute in her late teens. Must be nonsmoker."

I went to the Missing Persons' Bureau. No one was there.

Beethoven was so hard of hearing he thought he was a painter.

I choose toilet paper through a process of elimination.

Meow means "woof" in cat.

On Thanksgiving, you realize you're living in a modern world. Millions of turkeys baste themselves in millions of ovens that clean themselves.

A day off is always more welcome when it is unexpected.

Some people see things that are and ask, Why? Some people dream of things that never were and ask, Why not? Some people have to go to work and don't have time for all that shit.

RIDE THE WILD PARAMECIUM

How can everyone's money be "hard-earned," and everyone's vacation be "well-deserved"? Sounds like bullshit to me.

What exactly is "diddley squat"?

We now buy watches primarily for their looks, price, or additional functions. The fact that they tell time seems lost.

I think you ought to be able to lease a dog.

I don't understand the particular importance of remembering where you were when JFK was assassinated. I remember where I was a lot of times.

What year did Jesus think it was?

There's a new lottery game called Blotto. You get drunk and pick the numbers.

With all this natural selection going on, why doesn't the human race get any smarter? Is this it? Why are there still so many stupid people? Apparently, being a real dumb jackoff has some survival value.

Why is there always a small hole near the tip of a pen?

I enjoy going to a party at one of the Kennedys' homes, dropping to the floor, and yelling, "Hit the deck, he's got a gun!"

You know what disease you never hear about? Cancer of the heart.

LIFE IS A NEAR-DEATH EXPERIENCE

Amy Vanderbilt, the foremost authority on etiquette, commited suicide and apparently didn't have the courtesy to leave a note.

If the bouncer gets drunk, who throws *him* out?

The world began going downhill when ticket-takers in movie theaters stopped wearing uniforms.

When primitive people practice the rain dance, does it rain at the end of practice? And if it doesn't, how do they know they did the dance correctly?

The original Shick Smoking Centers were very primitive. They gave you one lecture and then you came back a week later. If they smelled tobacco on your breath, they beat the shit out of you.

If you live to be a hundred, your lucky number goes up by one.

FUCK THE
MIDDLE CLASS

Medical Progress: The medical profession is only now beginning to concede that maybe, just maybe, nutrition has something to do with good health. And that maybe, just maybe, the mind is somehow mysteriously linked to the body. Of course, there's not much money in such thinking.

If you mail a letter to your mailman, will he get it before he's supposed to?

I enjoy watching a woman with really bad teeth and a good sense of humor struggling to use her lips and tongue to hide her teeth when she's laughing. I just stand there and tell her joke after joke after joke.

Never tell a Spanish maid you want everything to be spic-and-span.

President Bush declared a National Day of Prayer for Peace. This was some time after he had carefully arranged and started the war.

They keep saying you can't compare apples and oranges. I can. An apple is red and distinctly non-spherical; an orange is orange and nearly spherical. So, what's the big problem?

After a big flood, where do all those rowboats go?

The Chinese have a saying: On a journey of a thousand miles, 512 is a little more than half.

McDonald's "breakfast for under a dollar" actually costs much more than that. You have to factor in the cost of coronary bypass surgery.

I don't like to lose my bearings, so I keep them in the cabinet near my bed.

When Popeye blows through his pipe, why doesn't he get sprayed with burning ash?

George Washington's brother was the Uncle of Our Country.

If you fall asleep on the couch in a house where a woman is present, there will be a blanket or a coat covering you when you awaken.

Politics is so corrupt even the dishonest people get fucked.

When blowing out your birthday candles, suppose you wish for one candle to stay lit? Is it possible for your wish to come true?

MY FIRST NINE DOGS ARE DEAD

I got a chest X-ray last month, and they found a spot on my lung. Fortunately it was barbecue sauce.

When a masochist brings someone home from the bar, does he say, "Excuse me a moment, I'm going to slip into something uncomfortable?"

This year is the two-millionth anniversary of sperm.

When you pick something up with your toes and transfer it to your hand, don't you feel, just briefly, like a superior creature? Like you could probably survive alone in a forest for a long time? Just briefly.

If all our national holidays were observed on Wednesdays, we might conceivably wind up with nine-day weekends.

The day after tomorrow is the third day of the rest of your life.

Why must hailstones always be the size of something else? And if it must be that way, why don't they have hailstones the size of testicles?

Cloud nine gets all the publicity, but cloud eight actually is cheaper, less crowded, and has a better view.

It is bad luck to kill a dog with a cooking spoon.

don't you love these people who end their sentences with a rising inflection? And they do it all the time? As though it were an intelligent way to talk? And everything they say sounds like a question? Even the answers? "How are you today?" "I'm fine?"

The swallows know that on the nineteenth of March the tourists come back to Capistrano.

What's all this stuff about retirement I keep hearing on TV commercials? People planning, saving; they can't wait to retire. One woman on TV says to her husband, "At this rate, Jeff, we'll never be able to retire!" What is this all about? Why would someone spend his whole life doing something he can't wait to get away from?

One of my favorite things in the movies is seeing a person hanged.

DON'T GET YOUR CORTEX CAUGHT IN A VORTEX

I often think how different the world would be if Hitler had not been turned down when he applied to art school.

Don't you get tired of these cereal commercials where they show the milk being poured in slow motion, and it splashes off a raspberry?

I enjoy watching people in rush-hour traffic. Thousands of them, stressed, frustrated, hurrying to and from their chosen places of enslavement. It's especially enjoyable from an airplane, because you can see their houses as well. The houses, like the people, all the same. Towns and subdivisions all the same. Cul de sacs. Like their lives, going nowhere. "Not a through street."

I think they should lower the drinking age. I just want to see a sign in a bar that says, You Must Be 11 and Prove It.

Positive thinking doesn't sound like a very good idea to me. I'm sure it doesn't work. And if it does, it's probably real hard to do.

Sometimes when I watch a parade, I wonder how many of the marchers are in desperate need of a good long piss.

So far, the Ku Klux Klan has not produced any really great composers.

THINK CLOWN
VOMIT

Tomorrow is very much like today, except it's not here yet.

I admire a man who drives clear across town to a distant shopping center where no one knows him, and rides all afternoon on the children's coin-operated "horsie."

My fondest wish is that I learn to write a capital "X" in longhand without lifting the pen from the paper.

Always be careful what you say. Nathan Hale said,"I only regret that I have but one life to give for my country." They killed him.

The difference between the blues and the blahs is that you can't sing the blahs.

I find the high five repulsive. It's typical lame, suburban white-boy bullshit. Any "five" that takes place above the waist is lame white-boy bullshit. I sincerely hope these high fives are causing long-term arm and shoulder injuries.

DOES GOD REALLY HAVE TO
WATCH ALL THIS SHIT?

Bus lag: a low-level disorientation caused by riding on a bus. Almost impossible to detect.

long before man discovered fire, he had sand and water to put it out with.

When you look at some of Picasso's paintings, it makes you wonder what kind of women he visualized when he masturbated.

Cancer is caused by a fear of malignant tumors.

honesty may be the best policy, but it's important to remember that, apparently, by elimination, dishonesty is the second best policy. Second is not all that bad.

You don't meet many Japanese guys named Biff.

We use the sun to make electricity, and then we use the electricity to operate sun lamps and tanning machines.

I'm unusual in one respect. My lucky number is 541,633.

A laugh is a smile with a hole in it.

People in the central and mountain time zones are getting too much sleep. Their late news comes on at 10 P.M., an hour earlier than in coastal time zones, and yet the morning talk shows come on at 7 A.M., the same as the rest of the country. So, central and mountain people are getting an extra hour's sleep. I think it makes them sluggish.

I NEVER LIKED A MAN I DIDN'T MEET

Preparation H is also good for a fat lip.

It's annoying to have a song running through your mind all day that you can't stop humming. Especially if it's something difficult like "Flight of the Bumblebee."

'Il bet you and I are a lot alike. Did you ever get together with a bunch of people and hang someone? Isn't it awful? You just want the guy's body to stop spasming. Every time I do it, I say, "This is absolutely the last time I'm doin' this." And still I go back.

Most people work just hard enough not to get fired and get paid just enough money not to quit.

I recently read that some guy had killed his girlfriend. You know, it's always been my contention that at the moment you decide to kill your girlfriend, that decision is tantamount to breaking off the relationship. Therefore, at the time you kill the person in question she is actually no longer your girlfriend.

In reverse order, our last eight presidents: A hillbilly wilh a permanent hard-on; an upper-class bureaucrat-twit; an actor-imbecile; a born-again Christian peanut farmer; an unelected college football lineman; a paranoid moral dwarf; a vulgar cowboy criminal; and a mediocre playboy sex fiend.

I heard that crime has increased so much it is now a growth industry. My worry is that if it continues to grow at the current rate it will attract the criminal element.

I read that a Detroit man and his friend were arrested because they had forced the man's five-year-old son to smoke cigarettes, drink alcohol, and perform oral sex on them. Can you imagine? Cigarettes!

In New York State a fourteen-year-old can get married but he can't drive, so he is forced to go on his honeymoon on a bicycle or a skateboard.

SURF'S DOWN FOREVER

there is something refreshingly ironic about people lying on the beach contracting skin cancer, in an attempt to acquire a purely illusory appearance of good health while germ-laden medical waste washes up on the sand all around them.

The New Testament is not new anymore; it's thousands of years old. It's time to start calling it The Less Old Testament.

I saw a fast-food commercial where they were selling a sandwich made of pork fat dipped in butter and egg yolk, deep-fried in lard, wrapped in bacon, and topped with cheddar cheese. They call it "Plaque on a Bun."

Crooked judges live on fixed incomes.

In the drugstore, how do you know if you're buying a sundry, a notion, or an incidental?

Prefix has no suffix, but *suffix* has a prefix.

I have no sympathy for single dads. They got into their marriages because they wanted steady pussy. Steady pussy leads to babies. After the novelty wears off, the marriage goes away. Single dads. Big fuckin' deal.

"It's neither here nor there." Well, folks, it's gotta be somewhere. I certainly don't have it.

If a really stupid person becomes senile, how can you tell?

germany lost World War II because Hitler was completely distracted by ill-fitting clothing that he was constantly adjusting during the last two years of the war.

The best example of a housekeeper is a divorced woman.

I read somewhere that in the last census 1.6 percent of the people were not counted. How can they know that?

MRS. GOODWRENCH IS A LESBIAN

blow your nose" is an interesting phrase. Because you don't really *blow* your nose, you blow out *through* your nose. If you blew your nose, I think they'd put you away. You might get someone *else* to blow your nose, but he would have to be a really close friend. Or completely drunk.

Just when I began to find myself, depersonalization came in.

I enjoy making people feel uncomfortable. Walking down the jetway to board my plane I'll often turn to a stranger and say, "Boy, I sure hope we don't crash into a cornfield today. If we *do* go down in flames, I hope we hit some houses. Or a school."

When are they gonna come up with some new Christmas carols?

You know you're getting old when you begin to leave the same smell in the bathroom your parents did.

Isn't it interesting that only sex and excretion can be found legally obscene in this country? Not violence, not neglect, not abuse of humans. Only shitting and fucking; two of nature's most necessary functions and irresistible forces. We're always trying to control and thwart nature, even in our language. Fuck that shit!

You show me something that doesn't cause cancer, and I'll show you something that isn't on the market yet.

Grown-ups have great power. They can order candy on credit over the telephone and have it delivered. Wow.

Heart disease changed my eating habits, but I still cook bacon just for the smell.

It has become very easy to buy a gun. It used to be, "I have a gun, give me some money." Now it's, "I have some money, give me a gun."

YOU ARE ALL DISEASED

If you ever meet twins, talk to just one of them. It drives the other one crazy.

to promote their hog-raising industry, each year the state of Iowa selects a young woman and names her Pork Queen. How would you like to tell the guys down at the gas station that your daughter is the Pork Queen?

What exactly is "viewer discretion"? If viewers had discretion, most television shows would not be on the air.

Someday I wanna see the Pope come out on that balcony and give the football scores.

A seven-day waiting period for purchasing a handgun is stupid. It just gives the buyer that much more time to think of people he'd like to kill. Now, instead of a single murder, you've got a multiple homicide on your hands.

Have you ever become suddenly, intensely aware of your legs?

OUR ONLY HOPE IS INSANE LEADERSHIP

Remember, inside every silver lining there's a dark cloud.

for the last twenty-five years I've done over one hundred shows a year, each one attended by about two thousand people. More than five million people in all. I often wonder if anyone was ever killed while driving to or from one of my shows. If so, I blame myself.

Where is this guy Christo when I need something wrapped at Christmas?

I'm not worried about guns in school. You know what I'm waitin' for? Guns in church! That's gonna be a lotta fun.

If you look around carefully the next time you go out, you'll notice that there are some really fucked-up-looking people walking around.

Dogs lead a nice life. You never see a dog with a wristwatch.

When you close your eyes and rub real hard, do you see that checker-board pattern?

If cockpit voice recorders are so indestructible, why don't they just build an airplane that's one big cockpit voice recorder?

GOOD NEWS: Ten golfers a year are hit by lightning.

in a trial, if they break for lunch during someone's testimony, they always remind him afterward that he's still under oath. That means that all during lunch he was sworn to tell the truth. So, if someone asks him, "How's the soup?" he better be goddamn sure he gives an honest answer. "How's the soup?" "Objection! Calls for a conclusion!"

I've been working on accepting my inner scumbag.

How do they get all those Down's syndrome kids to look the same?

Santa is *satan* spelled inside out.

Don't you lose faith in your dog's intelligence when he takes a piss and then steps in it?

There was no Big Bang. There was just a Big Hand Job.

At my supermarket, I get on a checkout line marked "no items," and pay for things other people forgot to buy.

My favorite country song is, "I Shoulda Fucked Old What's-Her-Name."

One consolation about memory loss in old age is that you also forget a lot of things you didn't intend to remember in the first place.

There's actually something called the Table Tennis Hall of Fame.

Sometimes, during a big funeral that's being shown on TV, you'll see some really good-looking female mourners. But they never keep the cameras on them long enough to get a good careful look. And you can't see their eyes because a lot of times they're wearing sunglasses. It's frustrating. I happen to be particularly attracted to grief-stricken women.

THE DODGERS
EAT SHIT

What year in world history do you suppose the first person with really clean fingernails appeared?

What exactly is "midair"? Is there some other part of air besides the "mid" part?

Singing is basically a form of pleasant, controlled screaming.

The sound of one hand clapping is the same as the sound of a tree falling in the forest when no one is there to hear it.

What clinic did Betty Ford go to?

Wouldn't it be weird if the only way people could die was that their heads suddenly exploded without warning? If there was simply no other cause of death? One day you'd be sitting there having a hot chocolate, and suddenly your head would explode. You know something? I'll bet people would get used to it.

You know what they don't have? Cake-flavored pie.

I'd like to live in a country where the official motto was, "You never know." It would help me relax.

I can't wait until we get a really evil president. Not devious and cunning like Nixon and Johnson. But really, really evil. God, it would be so refreshing!

You know you're getting old when, after taking a leak, you shake your dick and dust comes out.

I avoid any restaurant that features Kaopectate on draft.

banks tell you to maintain a "minimum balance." I first learned about minimum balance from my uncle. He would come over to our house, drink a quart of wine, and try to stand up. That was minimum balance.

ANOTHER CRETIN FOR PEACE

Every now and then, on a certain days, in the late afternoon the air takes on a weird kind of purply, rose-colored light. What is that?

The neutron bomb is very Republican; it leaves property alone and concentrates on destroying large numbers of people indiscriminately.

being a comedian, I would love to see a production of *Hamlet* that included a drummer, so they could use rim shots to highlight the really good lines. "To be or not to be. That is the question." Ba-dum-bum!

I have no problem with the cigar smoking trend. If some guy wants to put a big, steaming turd in his mouth and suck on it, who am I to complain?

Why are we so surprised when terrorists manage to get a bomb on an airplane? Drug traffickers get things on airplanes all the time.

When you reach a certain age there comes a time when everyone you know is sick.

how can people take the Olympics seriously? Judges vote politically, athletes cheat on drugs, xenophobes run wild, and the whole thing is one big greed-driven logo competition.

Somehow, it's hard to picture butterflies fucking.

Do you know the nicest thing about looking at a picture of a 1950's baseball park? The only people wearing baseball caps are the players.

A deaf-mute carrying two large suitcases has rendered himself speechless.

It's way beyond ironic that a place called the Holy Land is the location of the fiercest, most deeply felt hatred in the world. And it makes for wonderful theater.

Whenever I see a picture of the General Assembly of the United Nations, I wonder how many of the delegates are whacked on drugs.

With all the cars, buses, trucks, airplanes, electric motors, gasoline engines, diesel engines, compressors, turbines, drills, fans, pumps, and generators running all the time, shouldn't the Earth now be making a loud humming sound as it moves around the sun?

The pores in a latex condom are one micron in size. The human immunodeficiency virus is one half micron. So, what's all this stuff about safe sex?

Mall walking. How perfect! Staying fit without having to take your eyes off the merchandise that got you out of shape in the first place.

I'm sixty, and I don't need child-resistant caps on my medicine bottles. They say, "Well, someone with children might come and visit you." Fuck 'em! They're on their own. Let 'em take their chances. Anyone who visits me is accepting a certain level of risk in the first place.

Can you imagine the increase in violence there would be if no one could lie? If we could all read each other's minds? Also, think of all the additional crying there would be.

A pager is an electronic leash, the better for your controllers to control you. One more sign that your life belongs to someone else.

Forty-five million people go to national parks each year. To get away from the other two hundred million.

Always do whatever's next.

That invisible hand of Adam Smith's seems to offer an extended middle finger to an awful lot of people.

If you want to know how fucked up the people in this country are, just look at television. Not the programs, not the news. The commercials. Just watch only the commercials for about a week, and you'll see how fucked up the people in this country really are.

theater and sports are similar, with minor differences: In theater, after rehearsing, the actors leave dressing rooms in costume to perform shows on stages in front of audiences. In sports, after practicing, the athletes leave locker rooms in uniform to play games on fields in front of spectators. And although it's true that both fields have agents, only the theater has makeup.

Sooner or later, your parents die.

Why do they put a suicide watch on certain death row prisoners? Why would you care if a man you're planning to kill kills himself? Does it spoil the fun? I also think about the death row prisoner in Texas who, on the day before his execution, managed to take a drug overdose. They rushed him to a hospital, saved his life, then brought him back to prison and killed him. Apparently, just to piss him off.

For many years, the Grand Ole Opry did not allow drums onstage.

ife has changed. The stores around the corner from my house used to be a grocer, butcher, laundry, tailor, barber shop, shoe repair, dry cleaner, and a beauty salon. Now it's a wig parlor, karate school, off-track betting, a software store, sushi, yogurt, video rentals, an adult bookstore, a T-shirt shop, a copying and printing center, a storefront law office, and a clothing store for fat women.

Sometimes, a city describes itself as a "Metroplex." This is one of those bull-shit word formations whereby a community tries to sound forward and progressive, in spite of all the evidence to the contrary.

After every horror, we're told, "Now the healing can begin." No. There is no healing. Just a short pause before the next horror.

I think once people reach the age of forty they should be barred from using the words *girlfriend* or *boyfriend* in reference to someone they're fucking. It's creepy.

Attention, all camouflaged males: In the American Revolution, the militias broke and ran from battle. They ran home. Only the regular army stood fast.

RULES TO LIVE BY

Life is not as difficult as people think; all one needs is a good set of rules. Since it is probably too late for you, here are some guidelines to pass along to your children.

1. Relax and take it easy. Don't get caught up in hollow conceits such as "doing something with your life." Such twaddle is outmoded and a sure formula for disappointment.

2. Whatever it is you pursue, try to do it just well enough to remain in the middle third of the field. Keep your thoughts and ideas to yourself and don't ask questions. Remember, the squeaky wheel is the first one to be replaced.

3. Size people up quickly, and develop rigid attitudes based on your first impression. If you try to delve deeper and get to "know" people, you're asking for trouble.

4. Don't fall for that superstitious nonsense about treating people the way you would like to be treated. It is a transparently narcissistic approach, and may be the sign of a weak mind.

5. Spend as much time as you can pleasing and impressing others, even if it makes you unhappy. Pay special attention to shallow manipulators who can do you the most harm. Remember, in the overall scheme, you count for very little.

6. Surround yourself with inferiors and losers. Not only will you look good by comparison, but they will look up to you, and that will make you feel better.

7. Don't buy into the sentimental notion that everyone has short-comings; it's the surest way of undermining yourself. Remember, the really best people have no defects. If you're not perfect, something is wrong.

8. If by some off chance you do detect a few faults, first, accept the fact that you are probably deeply flawed. Then make a list of your faults and dwell on them. Carry the list around and try to think of things to add. Blame yourself for everything.

9. Beware of intuition and gut instincts, they are completely unreliable. Instead, develop preconceived notions and don't waver unless someone tells you to. Then change your mind and adopt their point of view. But only if they seem to know what they're talking about.

10. Never give up on an idea simply because it is bad and doesn't work. Cling to it even when it is hopeless. Anyone can cut and run, but it takes a very special person to stay with something that is stupid and harmful.

11. Always remember, today doesn't count. Trying to make something out of today only robs you of precious time that could be spent daydreaming or resting up.

12. Try to dwell on the past. Think of all the mistakes you've made, and how much better it would be if you hadn't made them. Think of what you should have done, and blame yourself for not doing so. And don't go easy. Be really hard on yourself.

13. If by chance you make a fresh mistake, especially a costly one, try to repeat it a few times so you become familiar with it and can do it easily in the future. Write it down. Put it with your list of faults.

14. Beware also of the dangerous trap of looking ahead; it will only get you in trouble. Instead, try to drift along from day to day in a meandering fashion. Don't get sidetracked with some foolish "plan."

15. Finally, enjoy yourself all the time, and do whatever you want. Don't be seduced by that mindless chatter going around about "responsibility." That's exactly the sort of thing that can ruin your life.

YOU KNOW?

When you're young, you don't know, but you don't know you don't know, so you take some chances. In your twenties and thirties you don't know, and you *know* you don't know, and that tends to freeze you; less risk taking. In your forties you *know*, but you don't know you know, so you may still be a little tentative. But then, as you pass fifty, if you've been paying attention, you know, and you know you know. Time for some fun.

HAVE A LITTLE FUN

Most people take life much too seriously and worry about all the wrong things: security, advancement, prosperity, all those things that give you heartburn. I think people would be better off if they relaxed and had a little more fun.

Think about it: We're all here on a big rock, zippin' around a bad star for no good reason. We don't know where we came from, we don't know where we're going, we don't know how long it's gonna last, and we keep having to go to the bathroom. And on top of that, the whole thing is completely meaningless.

Do you ever stop to think about that? It's all meaningless. All this detail. What's it for? This table. What's it doing here? What's the purpose? Who cares? I think the whole thing is someone's idea of a great big practical joke. So, relax that extra-tight American anal sphincter, folks, and have a little fun. Here are some suggestions:

In a public restroom, stand on the toilet and stare over the top of the partition at the man in the next stall. Tell him your therapist told you it's a good way of relaxing. Then lean out of the stall with your pants down, and ask someone if you can borrow a set of chopsticks and a ninc-volt battery.

When you're out on the country-club dance floor with your wife, guide her over toward the orchestra and say to the conductor, "Tonight is our anniversary. Do you guys know 'Wong Has the Largest Tong in China'?"

Did you ever see these people who drive with their headlights on in the daytime, because they think it's safer? You know what would be fun? To smash head-on into a guy like that, just to show him that his idea doesn't work.

On the hotel "How-did-we-do?" form, write, "The maid offered to blow me for some candy," and "The room service waiter thrust his hand down my pants and manipulated my schwanz."

Here's some fun: At a taxi stand, give the first driver fifty dollars and tell him, "Go to the airport, and wait there for me." Then go to the second driver, give him fifty dollars and tell him, "Follow that cab, and under no circumstances allow it to get to the airport!" Then get in the third cab and tell the guy to follow the other two. When you're about halfway to the airport, take out a gun and start shooting at the first two cabs. Yell, "Hi-yo, Silver!" a lot.

Go into a store and tell the clerk you don't want to purchase anything. Then ask him if he'd be interested in buying sixty gallons of children's urine.

Next time you're on a plane, sit in the back row and place a boom box under your seat. Then, during takeoff, play high-pitched, metal-grinding noises on it, just loud enough to be heard over the engines. If possible, blend in the sound of a few small, muffled explosions. Keep saying, "Uh-oh!"

While seated at a nice dinner party, take a long look at the china service and say, "Hey, we had these same dishes in the army!"

Rush up to a hotel desk and mumble to the clerk, "Did the purple man with the dwarf in the cardboard box leave the Archbishop's phone number?" He will say, "What?" Repeat the sentence a little more loudly, but keep it hard to understand. Once again, a little annoyed, he will say, "What?" Keep this up until he reaches the breaking point and a small gathering of foam has appeared at the corner of his mouth. Then, when his supervisor comes over to inquire, tell her innocently, "I don't know what the problem is, ma'am. I simply asked this gentleman how late the restaurant is open, and he flew off the handle."

At a retail store, make a lot of large purchases hurriedly, and then, when signing the credit card slip, appear nervous and openly try to copy the signature that appears on your credit card. Then when the approval comes through, express visible relief. "Really? All right!!" Snicker a little, and mutter a barely audible, "Idiots."

HITCHHIKING FUN

There are some people who still hitchhike, although not as many as before. A lot of folks gave the practice up after being buried in shallow graves near the side of the road. But here's some fun you can have in case you still like to get out and hoist a thumb. Of course, you have to get a ride first. Someone has to stop.

When the guy says, "Where you going?" lean way into the car and bellow, "Turn this thing around, Zeke, I'm headin' back the other way!" Then make sure to step back quickly. No sense being dragged five hundred yards for the sake of a joke.

Or, when the guy stops, don't say anything; just jump in and sit down. When he says, "Where you going?" say, "I don't give a shit. Let's just ride around. I'm off till Thursday." Then make a lot of motor noises with your mouth.

Here's another good one: "Thanks for stopping. I don't actually need a ride today, but if you'd give me your phone number, I'd be glad to let you know when I *do*. It'll save you the trouble of driving all around looking for me." Once again, stepping back quickly might prevent a base case of gravel burn.

This one is my favorite. Guy stops, lowers the window and says, "Where you going?" You say, "Well . . . first we gotta go pick up my mother. Then we gotta go to the abortionist, the meth dealer, and the ammo shop. Then we gotta take her home. She lives in Indiana. By the way, do you know how to change a colostomy bag?"

So, have a little fun. Soon enough you'll be dead and burning in Hell with the rest of your family.

L'CHAIM!

If somehow you manage not to be canceled out by birth control pills, IUDs or condoms, and you are actually conceived; and then by some additional stroke of luck you are not aborted, miscarried, or given a birth defect by your mother's use of tobacco, alcohol, speed, heroin, or crack; and you are lucky enough to be born as a relatively normal child, then all you have to worry about is being beaten or sexually abused for your first 16 years. After that, you have a chance, at least a chance, of being chronically unemployed or killed in a war.

FIRST i WAS A kiD

I'm sixty years of age. That's 16 Celsius. And I've never told you much about my childhood.

It seems I was unusual even before I was born. During pregnancy, my mother carried me very low. Indeed, for the last six weeks, my feet were sticking out. She was the only woman in the neighborhood who had maternity shoes. But she told me I was a big help when it came to climbing stairs.

I was a healthy baby, except for one ear that's folded and a little bent. The doctor said it happened because, apparently, at the precise moment I was being conceived, my mother and father fell off the hood of the car.

My parents chose what, at that time, was the very latest method of childbirth. You've heard of Lamaze? This was La Paz. The mother receives powerful narcotics, the father is sent to Bolivia, and the nurse does all the screaming.

As soon as I was born, I noticed that babies have it pretty easy: Wake up, cry, piss, roll over, drool, suck, eat, gag, belch, puke, giggle, crap, crawl, stand, fall, cry, scream, bleed, coo, sleep . . . and dream.

I went through the usual stages: imp, rascal, scalawag, whippersnapper. And, of course, after that it's just a small step to full-blown sociopath. I'm probably the only child who went directly from shenanigans to crimes against nature.

I was always a little different. Most kids had a dog named Spot. You know what I called my dog? Stain. Different. Instead of my thumb, I sucked my ring finger. And I had a strange ambition: I just wanted to live longer than Jesus. My mother said it was because I was sensitive, so she washed me in Woolite.

I was a hip kid. When I saw Bambi it was the midnight show. My cap gun had a silencer. My lemonade stand had dance hostesses. And one night at dinner, when I was about ten, I leaned over to my father and said, "Hey, man, when are we gonna load up on some of that breast milk again?" Still, I was practical. When one of my playmates died in an accident, I asked his mother if I could have his toys.

As a boy I was negatively affected by two things. First of all, I grew up on the side of a very steep hill. I think that can throw you off. Here's another thing: When you look at a map lying on a table, north is usually the direction pointing away from you. But my front door faced south, so you can see, as soon as I left my house, everything was backward. Things like that have an effect.

There's one other thing I should mention: You know how when you're real little your dad will throw you up in the air and catch you? Well, one day my dad threw me up in the air, and I went so high I could see the curvature of the earth. I believe I even caught a glimpse of Sri Lanka. At the time, of course, it was still called Ceylon. Dad and I had no idea its name would change someday. Anyway, after he threw me up in the air, he didn't wait around. He walked away. They said after that I was never really the same. They would whisper, "The boy is no longer playin' with a full bag of jacks!"

What happened was I became a loner; I just wanted to be by myself. I had an imaginary friend, but I didn't bother with him. Fuck 'im! Let him get his own friends. I got no time for people like that.

When you're a loner, of course, you have to make up your own games. Tag was difficult.

I used to play Cop. And instead of Hide and Seek, I would play a pathetic little game called Hide. One time I remained hidden for over a month before I realized that no one was looking for me. It was sad, really. But there are compensations. To this day, I remain unchallenged at Musical Chair.

My mother would say, "Why are you always playing alone?" And I would say, "I'm not playin', Ma. I'm fuckin' serious!" They first noticed I was strange when I insisted on listening to the circus on the radio. I guess I was a bad boy. Besides shitting in my pants, I would also shit in other people's pants.

Eventually, she sent me to a child psychologist. It was all the vogue at the time. So I went, and I honestly believe he was crazier than I was. I should've stabbed him many times in the eyes with a railroad spike when I still had the chance. I consider it a lost opportunity.

One problem was that my mother was very strict, and on top of that she was a physically imposing woman. Thinking back, the person she most reminds me of is Charles Kurault. I didn't really like her. I can remember staring at the orphanage and feeling envy.

Of course, it wasn't all bad; there are pleasant memories, too. Every Sunday after church, my mother and I would buy the Sunday papers and walk home together. Then she'd get drunk and try to make pancakes.

In a way, I take all the blame. I was hard to handle, and it wasn't easy on her. As I said, I'm sixty now, and she still isn't over her postpartum depression. And yet, she's a typical mom; she still tells me I'm going to be tall. And, you know something? Her wish is coming true. She's getting smaller. Soon I will be, too.

I guess the thing I miss most about childhood is riding piggyback, and here's something I don't tell too many people: I still like to ride piggyback occasionally. I really do. And I don't mean across the room. I'm talking about long trips. I went to Florida last winter. Piggyback. Fortunately, I have very indulgent friends. And I pay top dollar.

SCHOOL DAYS

As far as school was concerned, I did pretty well, if you don't count learning. My problem was, during the summer I would forget everything they had taught the year before. So, basically, when September rolled around, I was back to square one. The teachers told me, "You have an excellent mind. It just isn't readily apparent to an outside observer."

One of my problems was lying. I always got caught, because I told big lies. One morning, late for school, I told the teacher I'd had to iron my own shirt, because my parents had been strangled by a telephone lineman.

Actually, I was much too logical for school. For instance, after about a month in first grade, the teacher asked me something, and I said, "Why are you asking *me* these questions? I came here to learn from you."

They would try to keep me after school, but I knew my rights. Once again, logic: I told them, "When school is out, and the students have all gone home, this building is technically no longer a school. It becomes just another building, and you have no right to keep me in it." Staying after school wasn't actually all that bad. At least there wasn't any learning going on.

But it wasn't easy to learn in my school even during normal hours. Because we were a poor area, the school had a small budget and was unable to teach the second half of the alphabet. And so, to me, anything past the letter *m* is still pretty much a mystery. The Renaissance, the Reformation, Reconstruction. When these topics come up, I have no idea what people are talking about.

And so, I volunteered for being silly. I did so as soon as I discovered it was an option. One day, the teacher interrupted something I was doing and said, "Mister Carlin, you can either take responsibility and learn this material, or you can continue to act silly." Well, that was all I needed to hear.

It turned out I was pretty good in science. But again, because of the small budget, in science class we couldn't afford to do experiments in order to prove theories. We just believed everything. Actually, I think that class was called Religion. Religion was always an easy class. All you had to do was suspend the logic and reasoning you were being taught in all the other classes.

SPORTS, FIGHTING, AND GIRLS

I did better in sports, and was successful even before I entered school: As an infant, a particularly brutal uncle taught me full-contact pat-a-cake. I found it painful, but quite exhilarating. Later, in grammar school, I played intramural Simon Says and took several bronze medals in high-speed competition skipping.

I played basketball for three years, and when I left school, they retired my jersey. Primarily for reasons of hygiene. I wasn't a real stand-out at basketball, but I'm convinced that if I had been a lot taller, a lot faster, and had really good aim, I would have been a better player.

I wasn't much of a fighter, either. If a tough kid challenged me to a fight, I would make an excuse: "I'm not allowed to fight in this suit." Most of the time they would simply steal the suit. Which was fine with me, as I found I could run much faster in my underwear. I didn't have much of a "rep." They would say of me, "He can't dish it out, and he can't take it either."

The one time I did box, at camp, I fought as a walterweight: It turned out I was the exact same weight as my friend Walter. I lost my only bout. But I realize now it's probably just as well God didn't make me a good fighter, or else there'd have been a long trail of dead men across America.

Don't forget, I came from a pretty tough neighborhood. Not the toughest, maybe, but still fairly tough. You've heard of Hell's Kitchen? This was Hell's Dining Room. And we didn't live far from something really unusual, a tough rich neighborhood: Hell's Servants' Quarters.

We had some pretty tough characters. In fact, if Charles Bronson had lived in my neighborhood, he would've been a Playboy bunny. On Halloween, we would dress up funny and kill a person. And we always did things differently: Once a week, a bunch of us liked to get drunk and beat up heterosexuals. And although I broke a lot of laws as a teenager, I straightened out immediately upon turning eighteen, when I realized the state had a legal right to execute me.

It may surprise you that I wasn't very good with girls. Too smart. When I would play doctor, and "examine" a girl, I would often find an aneurysm. One time, in the midst of a particularly erotic physical exam, I discovered advanced hypertrophic cardiomyopathy. I continued to feel the girl up, of course, and only later, after reaching a private climax in my pants, did I inform her of my diagnosis. First things first. I can't tell you how many women over the years have written to thank me for finding a lump in their breasts.

My first girlfriend, however, was afraid of sex. Apparently, one night before falling asleep, she had been fondled by the sandman. As a result, she suffered recurring wet nightmares. I could sympathize with her, of course, as for years I had been the victim of wet daydreams. I realize now it was probably just as well God didn't make me a great lover, or else there'd have been a long trail of pregnant women all across America.

It was my uncle who taught me about the birds and the bees. He sat me down one day and said, "Remember this, George, the birds fuck the bees." Then he told me he once banged a girl so hard her freckles came off.

DR. BEN DOVER

Sooner or later, the young medical student has to tell his blue-collar father that he wants to be a proctologist:

"Wait a minute, Vinny, lemme get this straight. I busted my nuts for twenty years tryin' to save enough money to put you through college and now you tell me you want to stick your finger up a guy's ass?"

"Not finger, Dad. Hand!"

"Jesus!"

FUZZ BUSTER

Microwave radiation leaking from radar guns has caused at least eighty cases of testicular cancer in policemen. I'm glad. That's what they get for being sneaky. Cancer and radar both victimize silently; they sneak up on you. You think everything's OK, but unknown to you, something bad is happening. Then suddenly you're a victim. Also, it's quite appropriate that it's testicular cancer. These cops all think they have big balls. Now they do. Good.

LIGHTEN UP A LITTLE

Riot police sometimes use rubber bullets. Imagine! Someone, somewhere, had a lucid thought. And I think they might have provided a small opening here. This idea could be extended to larger weapons. Rubber bullets, naugahyde hand grenades, crushed velvet land mines, silk torpedoes, Nerf tanks, whiffle missiles. How about a neutron bomb made of fake fur?

They also have water cannons. Why not go further? How about cannons that shoot ginger ale? Skim milk? Orange juice from concentrate? And what unruly mob could possibly defy a police force armed with a vegetable soup cannon? Chunky style, of course.

And it's always struck me that our two most-used gasses produce only tears and laughter. How about a gas that creates crippling self-doubt? Or a gas that conjures up terrifying childhood memories? Okay, last one: How about a gas that fills you with an unquenchable desire for vanilla pudding?

BAG A BOOMER

I only hope that when the Generation Xers are finally running things, they'll have the courage to kill all these baby boomers, one by one, in their hospital beds and their nursing homes. Kill them and loot their pensions and estates, and throw them out into the streets with nothing. If they don't, the boomers will take everything they can and keep it for themselves. They're trying now to arrange for the next two generations to pay their debts, having already put young people deeply in hock. Boomers are living off their grandchildren's money and will try to steal everything else before they're gone.

If you young people want to know who to kill, I'll tell you. There are two schools of thought on this: Some say the baby boomers were born between 1946 and 1964. Others will tell you 1942 through 1960. Just to be on the safe side, I'd say kill everyone between the ages of thirty and fifty-five. The boomers used to say, "Don't trust anyone over thirty." Well, the stakes are a little higher now. So ask to see a driver's license and then strangle a boomer. That's my advice. I always like to have something uplifting to offer along with all the gloomy shit.

YOU GET NO CREDIT HERE

People should not get credit for having qualities they're supposed to have. Like honesty. What's the big deal anyway? You're *supposed* to be honest. It's not a skill.

Besides, people shouldn't get credit for skills in the first place. Do you think you should be praised for something you had no control over? I mean, if you were born with certain abilities and characteristics—things that are an essential part of your makeup—I don't see that you should be taking bows, do you? You couldn't help it; it was genetically encoded. No one deserves credit for being tall.

People say, "Well, talent can only get you so far. It still takes a lot of hard work." Yeah? Well, hard work is genetically encoded, too. Some people can't help working hard; it's enjoyable to them. They can no more remain idle than change the color of their eyes. People who work hard and display great talent do not deserve special praise. Quite often the credit should go to their grandparents. Or perhaps their grandparents' milkman.

Also, I don't understand why people who recover from illness or injury are considered courageous. Getting well should not be cause for praise. Just because someone is no longer sick doesn't mean they did something special. Getting well is a combination of seeking help, following advice, having a good attitude, and being the possessor of an effective immune system. All of these qualities stem from inborn genetic traits and characteristics. No one makes a conscious choice to be courageous. It's genetically encoded.

Believe me, when the only alternative is lying in a puddle of your own shit, it doesn't take much courage to get up and go to physical therapy. Courage comes into play when people have options, not when they're backed against a wall. It didn't take courage for Magic Johnson to announce he was HIV positive. He had no choice. Sooner or later people were going to find out. It was a matter of public relations, not courage.

And another type of courage, "bravery in battle," is to me even more suspect. Not only are there inherited genetic traits at work, there are also heavy doses of adrenaline and testosterone contributing to the situation, and those two hormones are affected and controlled by genes too. There are not really any heroes—there are only genetic freaks.

So relax, folks. The pressure's off. Everything's encoded. You heard it here.

BUNGEE THIS!

Remember the guy who paid one hundred dollars at a Michigan fair to try the bungee jump? And the cord broke, and he fell? The guy wanted his hundred dollars back. Is he kidding? I'd say, "Fuck you! You owe an extra hundred!" A hundred for goin' down, and a hundred for goin' down the rest of the way. Shit, he got twice the excitement, he oughta pay twice the price.

And they said he glanced off the side of the "air mattress." Air mattress? What kinda fuckin' bungee jump is that? Jagged rocks! That's what they oughta have at the bottom. If there's no risk, why bother? Fuckin' air mattress. My pulse wouldn't even change. If these guys are thrill seekers, let 'em seek a real thrill: I think every third bungee cord should be defective.

CHOW TIME ON DEATH ROW

Suppose you're on death row, and they tell you you can have one last meal. And it's an honorable thing, they take pride in it and they really try to live up to it. But you can't make up your mind. You have most of the meal figured out except you can't decide between steak and lobster. You honestly can't decide. Can they kill you? If you really can't decide? Truth serum, lie detector, psychologists; it becomes a big media thing: "MAN TELLING THE TRUTH. CAN'T REALLY DECIDE." Can they kill you? Can they honestly drag you down the last mile screaming, "Turf, surf, who knows?" But then, finally. Finally, after eighteen months of indecision, you say, "OK! I got it! Gimme the steak!" And everybody goes, "Ohh, cool, wow, he wants the steak." Then the warden says to you. "How would you like that steak done?" And you say, "Oh, Jeez . . . I have no idea. Can I get back to you on that?"

NUMBER FUN

If a picture is worth ten thousand words,* then one twenty-five-hundredth of a picture should be worth four words.

And if Helen of Troy had the face that launced a thousand ships, and a picture is worth ten thousand words, doesn't that mean one picture of Helen's face should be worth ten million ships?

And, if the night has a thousand eyes, and getting there is half the fun, that means to have fun getting there at night would require five hundred eyes.

And, if getting there is half the fun, and half a loaf is better than none, would getting halfway there with a whole loaf be more or less fun?

And if half a loaf is better than none, the night has a thousand eyes, a picture is worth ten thousand words, getting there is half the fun, and Helen of Troy had the face that launched a thousand ships,

*The actual proverb is "One picture is worth ten thousand words." —Confucius

then in a picture taken at night from a ship that is halfway there, how much fun would Helen be having if she were holding a full loaf? And could you see it in her eyes?

OK, now suppose Helen of Troy lived in a halfway house. . . .

SOMETHING'S MISSING

Why are there no B batteries? There aren't even any A batteries. In fact, it's almost as if they went out of their way to avoid A. They went straight to AA and AAA. Also, I never see any grade B milk, or type III audio cassettes. And there are no vitamins F, G, H, I, and J. Why? Why are certain airline seat numbers missing, and what ever became of the Boeing 717? And Chanel #4? Also, all I ever hear about are the Sixth and Seventh Fleets. Where are the other five? And why are there hardly any brown running shoes? Or green flowers? I dare not even mention blue food.

SCIENCE FRICTION

I'm gettin' sick of "scientific progress." Scientists are easily the least responsible class in society. If you're one of those "green" assholes who run around worrying about the condition of the planet all the time, you might as well just go ahead and blame it all on the scientists. They're the ones who fouled the nest. Without them, none of the bad shit gets done. Self-important, asshole scientists, most of them working for the Pentagon or big business, creating harmful products we don't need. They don't care what they produce as long as they get to publish their fuckin' papers.

And the idealistic ones? The ones who won't have anything to do with the weapons makers and greed-heads? The ones involved in "pure research"? They lay the groundwork for the truly dangerous scientists who move in later and apply the knowledge commercially. Scientists have consistently assaulted and violated your planet. That's why you have AIDS, that's why you have a hole in your ozone layer, that's why your atmosphere is overheating, that's why you have toxic and nuclear waste, and that's why everything has a thin coating of oil on it. And next, they're going to turn these irresponsible motherfuckers loose on human genetic engineering. That ought to be a real treat. Scientists. The only ones worth a fuck are theoretical physicists. At least they're nuts.

ANIMAL INSTINCTS

At the start, let me say I am not an animal rights activist. I'm not comfortable with absolutes.

And I know that every time something eats, something else dies. I recognize the Earth is little more than a revolving buffet with weather. So, the idea of eating animals is fine with me, but is it really necessary to make things out of the parts we don't eat? We're the only species that does this. You never see a mongoose with snakeskin shoes. Or a lion walkin' around in a wildebeest hat. And how often do you run into plankton that have phytoplankton luggage?

And I think people have a lot of nerve locking up a tiger and charging four dollars to let a few thousand worthless humans shuffle past him every day. What a shitty thing to do. Humans must easily be the meanest species on Earth. Probably the only reason there are any tigers left is because they don't taste good.

I respect animals. I have more sympathy for an injured or dead animal than I have for an injured or dead human being, because human beings participate and cooperate in their own undoing. Animals are completely innocent. There are no innocent human beings.

Here is an anecdote from the writer Patricia Highsmith: "Not so long ago I said to a friend of mine: 'If I saw a kitten and a little human baby sitting on the curb starving, I would feed the kitten first if nobody was looking.' My friend said: 'I would feed the kitten first if somebody *was* looking.'" I would too, Patricia.

Some people seem shocked and say, "You care more about animals than you do about humans!" Fuckin'-A well told!

I do not torture animals, and I do not support the torture of animals, such as that which goes on at rodeos: cowardly men in big hats abusing simple beasts in a fruitless search for manhood. In fact, I regularly pray for serious, life-threatening rodeo injuries. I wish for a cowboy to walk crooked, and with great pain, for the rest of his life.

I cheer when a bull at Pamplona sinks one of his horns deep into the lower intestines of some drunken European macho swine. And my cheers grow louder when the victim is a young American macho-jock tourist asshole. Especially if the bull is able to swing that second horn around and catch the guy right in the nuts.

But although I don't go out of my way to bother living things, I am not without personal standards. A mosquito on my arm, an ant or a cockroach in my kitchen, a moth approaching my lapel; these animals will die. Other insects in my home, however, the ones who merely wish to rest awhile, will be left alone. Or, if noisy and rowdy, lifted gently and returned to the great outdoors.

I am also perfectly willing to share the room with a fly, as long as he is patrolling that portion of the room that I don't occupy. But if he starts that smart-ass fly shit, buzzing my head and repeatedly landing on my arm, he is engaging in high-risk behavior. That's when I roll up the sports section and become Bwana, the great white fly hunter!

Sometimes there's an older fly in the room, one who flies slowly and can't travel too far in one hop–or it might be a female, heavy with eggs. In this case, even if the fly is bothering me, I don't kill it; instead, I adopt it as a short-term pet. I might even give it a name. Probably something based on mythology.

Generally, I like flies, but they'd be far more welcome if they would make a choice—and stick to it—between my bean burrito and that nice, hot, steaming dog turd out in the front yard.

Also, in keeping with my insect death policy based on the intentions of the insect, any bacterium or virus entering my body that does not wish me well will be slain. Normally, my immune system would accomplish this without notifying me, but if the old T-cells aren't up to the task, I am prepared to ingest huge amounts of antibiotics, even if they are bad for me.

And yet, in spite of all these examples of creature mayhem, I will not strike a dog, I will not chase and taunt a bull around a ring, and I will not squeeze an animal's testicles just to give the yokels a better show.

I'm also uneasy about the sheer number of scientific experiments performed on animals. First of all, animals are not always good models for medical experimentation: penicillin kills guinea pigs; an owl is not bothered by cyanide; monkeys can survive strychnine, etc., etc. Couldn't these scientific tests just as easily be performed on humans? Condemned prisoners, old people, the feeble, the terminally ill? I'm sure there are plenty of ignorant, desperate Americans who would be willing to volunteer in exchange for some small electrical appliance.

What makes me happy in the midst of all this is that ultimately animals get even. The major killers of humanity throughout recent history—smallpox, influenza, tuberculosis, malaria, bubonic plague, measles, cholera, and AIDS—are all infectious diseases that arose from diseases of animals. I pray that mad cow disease will come to this country and completely wipe out the hamburger criminals. Eating meat is one thing, but this whole beef-rancher-manure-cattle-hamburger side show is a different skillet of shit altogether.

Each year, Americans eat 38 billion hamburgers. It takes 2,500 gallons of water to produce one pound of red meat. Cattle consume one half of all the fresh water consumed on earth. The sixty million people who will starve this year could be adequately fed if Americans reduced their meat intake by just 10 percent. But if I were one of those sixty million people, I wouldn't be reachin' for the salt and pepper too quickly. It ain't gonna happen.

Ranchers raise pathetic, worthless cattle and sheep, animals who cannot live off the land without human supervision, and the same ranchers kill wolves, magnificent, individualistic animals fully capable of caring for themselves without assistance. Individualism gives way to sheep behavior. Sound familiar?

I root for a wolf to someday grab a rancher's kid. Yes I do. And you know something? The wolf would probably take the kid home and raise him, in the manner of Romulus and Remus; and probably do a better job than the rancher. Remember, wolves mate for life, and they care for their sick and infirm; they don't run them off, or kill them, or abandon them. Give me a wolf over some fuckin' jerkoff rancher any day of the week.

One last item to demonstrate the depth of human perversity: Some zoos now sell surplus animals to private hunting ranches where rich white men hunt them down and kill them for amusement.

No wonder they call it the *descent* of man.

GOOD DOGGIE

When your dogs lick a visitor and they say, "Oh, he's very affectionate," ask them, "Did you notice what he was doing prior to coming over and licking your face?" "No. Well, yes! I think he was cleaning himself. He's a very clean dog." "Well, his balls and asshole are very clean. In fact, he has a perfectly clean five-inch circle around his balls and asshole. His tongue, lips, and nose, however, are filthy with old dog shit and fermented ball sweat. Why do you think we taught him to shake hands?"

MOTHS AND LIGHTS

I don't like moths, because I can't predict their flight patterns. They don't seem to know where they're going. I don't like that.

And they're always hanging around light bulbs. Somehow they're even able to get inside the sealed light fixture between the bulb and the outer glass. How do they do that? One day you can clean out a hundred old, dead moths and then put the clean globe back on, and a month later there'll be another twenty or thirty full-grown dead moths inside the globe. How do they get in there?

And what is that attraction to light all about, anyway? You know what I think they're doing? Trying to read the writing on the light bulb. It's hard to read, isn't it? The writing on a light bulb is placed right where you can't read it when the light is on, because the light is too bright. And then, when the light is off, you can't read it, because there's not enough light. No wonder moths are so fucked up.

THE GEORGE CARLIN BOOK CLUB— "We've Got Books Out the Ass"

Offer #3: General Interest Titles

☐ *Twelve Things Nobody Cares About*

☐ *The Picture Book of Permanent Stains*

☐ *Firecracker in a Cat's Asshole: A Novel*

☐ *The Complete List of Everyone Who Enjoys Coffee*

☐ *The Official British Empire Registry of Blokes*

☐ *Ten Places No One Can Find*

☐ *Tits on the Moon* (science fiction)

☐ *Why Norway and Hawaii Are Not Near Each Other*

☐ *The History of Envy*

☐ *The Pus Almanac*

☐ *One Hundred People Who Are Only Fooling Themselves*

☐ *Diary of a Real Evil Prick*

☐ *Carousel Maintenance*

☐ *Why It Doesn't Snow Anymore*

☐ *The Dingleberry Papers*

✖ *A Treasury of Poorly Understood Ideas*

✖ *Why Jews Point*

✖ *The Golden Age of Tongue Kissing*

✖ *Famous Bullshit Stories of the Aztecs*

✖ *The Meaning of Corn*

✖ *Feel This: A Braille Sex Manual*

✖ *A Complete List of Everything That Is Still Pending*

✖ *Really Loud Singalongs for the Hard of Hearing*

GET A LIFE

One morning I get up, get out of bed, get showered, get some breakfast, and get to thinkin', "I'm not gettin' any." I get the urge to get some nookie, and get an idea. So I get dressed, get in my car, and get on the freeway.

When I get downtown, I get a few beers, get a buzz, and get lucky. I get a glimpse of a fine-looking woman. I get her a drink, get her talking, and we get acquainted. So I get up my courage and get her to agree to go get a room.

We get outta there, get some booze, get in a taxi, and get a hotel.

We get in the room, and get comfortable, and I'm gettin' excited 'cause I'm gonna get in her pants. So we get undressed, get in bed, and get started. And I'm gettin' hot 'cause she's gettin' horny. She wants to get down, and I wanna get my rocks off. I wanna get it up, get in, get it on, get off, and get out.

And it starts gettin' real good. But then I get thinking, "Suppose I get the clap? If I get the clap, I'll have to get shots. Might get worse. Could get AIDS. Shoulda got rubbers."

Now I get paranoid. Get a bit crazy. Get a bit scared.

Gotta get a grip.

Then it gets worse. Suppose she gets pregnant? Will she get an abortion? She might wanna get married. I can't get involved. If I gotta get married, I gotta get her a ring. How do I get it? I'd have to get credit. Or get hold of some money!

That means gettin' a job. Or gettin' a gun. And a getaway car. But suppose I get caught? Get busted by cops. Get thrown in the jail! Gotta get help. Get a good lawyer. Get out on bail.

No. I gotta get serious. Get it together. Get with the program. Get me a break, get me a job. Get a promotion, get a nice raise, get a new house, and get some respect. But if I get all of that, I can't get real cocky. Might get someone mad who'd get on my case, get me in trouble, and then I'd get fired.

Then I'd get mad, maybe get violent, get kicked outta work. Then get discouraged, start to get desperate, get hold of some drugs, get loaded, get hooked, and get sick. Get behind in my rent, get evicted, get thrown on the street.

Maybe get mugged, get beaten, get injured, get hospitalized, get operated on, get a blood clot, get a heart attack, get the last rites, get a stroke, get a flat line, get a trip to the graveyard, and get buried in a field.

So get this. You gotta get smart, and you gotta get real. Get serious. Get home, get undressed, get in bed, get some sleep. Or you might just get fucked. Get me?

A Few random sexual ejaculations

In spite of all the wonderfully entertaining sex crimes we enjoy in this country, Americans are still a prudish lot. So now we've decided to use the word *gender* when referring to a person's sex. Gender has been borrowed from linguistics, and will soon include other meanings: "I think he's perverted, Stan. He told me he had gender with a woodchuck." "He's as ugly as shit, Gloria, but the gender is strangely dark and quite intense." "Pull up your pants, Russell. I told you, anal gender is high-risk fun!" And, of course, that once-exciting 1960s tripod of sex, drugs, and rock 'n' roll has been completely euphemized. Now it's, "gender, controlled substances, and alternative rock."

If a movie is "R-rated," it means that if you're under seventeen, you have to see it with an adult:

"What's he doing, Dad?"

"He's fucking her, son."

SEX QUIZ FOR MEN:

1. Have you ever been walking on the street toward three great-looking women who all have fabulous tits, and you don't know which set of tits to stare at? And you only have a few seconds to decide? Thank God you can at least study their asses while they're walking away.

2. Did you ever see a really attractive mannequin in a department store, and you think maybe you'd like to fuck her? But you know you can't, so you try to sneak a quick look at

her crotch? And you don't worry about anyone seeing you, because they would never believe what you're thinking? Remember, ladies, the thought most often coursing through a man's mind is, "Boy, I'd sure like to fuck that."

3. Have you ever been talking to a married couple you just met, and the woman has really great tits? And you're dying to get a really long look at them, but you can't even take a quick glance, because her husband is staring right at you? Then, when he finally looks away for an instant, do you immediately look straight at her tits, regardless of whether or not it makes her uncomfortable?

News note: On TV recently, a guy was complaining that he was sexually "abused" by a female teacher when he was a boy. He said she touched him and made him touch her in their private parts. Yeah? So? Where's the abuse? Maybe I'm twisted or something, but as a child, I would've been willing to kill for this kind of special attention. I'd have had my hand in the air all day long, "Teacher! I need some more of that special help!" It would have really lent a stimulating new perspective to the idea of staying after school.

I'm glad I don't have any weird sexual fetishes. It's hard enough just getting laid, can you imagine cruising the bars searching for a submissive, albino rubber freak who wants you to throw canteloupes at his ass and shit on his chest?

I will, however, admit to being fascinated by a strange new perversion I've heard of. It's called S & W. Apparently just as you're about to come, your partner vomits root beer on you.

Actually, truth be known, my sexual fantasies are fairly prosaic: a woman takes off her dress, I fuck her, I drive home. Simple, neat, very little down side.

MARRY AN ORPHAN

Men, take my advice, marry an orphan. It's great. First of all, there are never any in-law problems. Second, there are no annoying Thanksgiving and Christmas visits sitting around pretending to enjoy the company of a couple of fifth-generation nitwits. In fact, when it comes to visiting her folks, the worst thing that might happen to you would be an occasional trip to the cemetery to leave some cheap flowers. And you might even get out of that by claiming a morbid fear of headstones.

But most important, as the relationship is just beginning, you won't have to worry about making a good impression on the girl's parents, nor will you have to get her father's approval. Believe me when I tell you, when you say, "I hope your father will approve of me," there is no greater thrill than having your beloved turn to you brightly and say, "My father's dead."

HAPPY NEW YEAR

How late in the new year can you say "Happy New Year" and not be considered weird? Actually, the whole thing starts on December 26. If on that day you think you're not going to see someone again until after New Year's, you wish them, "Happy New Year." And it's generally all right to say "Happy New Year" right on up through New Year's day. But after that, it begins to change a little. On January third or fourth, for instance, it still may be acceptable, but only if you haven't seen the person since the First. And then even as late as the sixth or seventh of January, you can still get away with it if you haven't seen the person for a really long time, say since Christmas. But once it starts gettin' into early April, if you're still running around telling people, "Happy New Year," you are simply begging to be fitted for one of those garments where the sleeves tie in the back. You are gonna wind up saying "Happy New Year" through that little food slot in the door. And no one, including you, will care what day it is. Or year, for that matter.

RHYMES YOU JUST DON'T HEAR IN SONGS ANYMORE

Easter/kiester

humor/tumor

Tonto/Toronto

surgery/perjury

manhandle/panhandle

nudist/Buddhist

postcard/Coast Guard

creditor/predator

pickup/hiccup

mobster/lobster

doormat/floormat

Eugene's/blue jeans

decaffeinated/decapitated

LOVE ME, LOVE MY SONG

There are entirely too many love songs. I know. Society probably demands a certain number of them, but, goddamn, is this the only thing people can sing about? As far as I'm concerned, the love song category is filled. Let's move on. There must be some other topics. Everything's a broken heart. "Broken heart. Broken heart." What about a broken rib cage? Hah? How would you like that? Or a ruptured spleen? You never hear a song about that. Wouldn't you like to see some nice tall woman with long hair and big tits up there beltin' out a song about a ruptured spleen? Or how about a nice song about a fire in a hotel? Or a guy who gets his legs caught in a threshing machine? How about someone who goes up into a hayloft and finds sixty dead Shriners? It seems to me we're passing up a lot of subjects that would make really good songs.

WHO'S TEACHING WHOM

What exactly is a "student teacher"? As I understand it, a student teacher is a person of student age who is far enough along in his education to be doing some teaching. But a "student teacher" could also be someone who simply teaches students, a *student* teacher. Which is what all teachers are.

Or a student teacher might be a student studying to become a teacher. Not yet a teacher, still a "student teacher." Such a student, studying to be a teacher, could also be called a "teaching student," which is, after all, what our original "student teacher" was: a teaching student.

Sometimes teachers, later in their careers, go back to school for further education, and once again they become students, while still remaining teachers. Well, if a younger student who is doing some teaching is a "student teacher," then wouldn't an older teacher who goes back to school logically be a "teacher student"? Or I guess you could call her a "student teacher," couldn't you? So far, that's three different kinds of student teachers.

Now, these teachers who go back to school obviously have to be taught by "teacher teachers." And if one of these teacher teachers were also taking a few courses on the side, that would make her a "student teacher teacher." And if she were just beginning that process, just learning to be a "student teacher teacher" wouldn't that make her a "student teacher teacher student"? I think it would.

CHANGING THE SUBJECTS

Talk about wrong priorities. We live in a country that has a National Spelling Bee. We actually give prizes for spelling! But when's the last time you heard about a thinking bee? Or a reasoning bee? Maybe an ethics bee? Never. Did you know the only people in our culture who are taught ethics are a handful of college students? Then they graduate and go to work for large corporations. So much for ethics training. Ethics and values should be taught early in grade school, not in college when the child has already been spiritually warped and perverted by his parents, friends, religion, and television set.

And while we're at it, why don't we teach courses in how to be responsible, or how to be married, or how to be a good parent, or, at the very least, how to be a reasonably honorable human being? Unfortunately, such courses will never be taught, because the information gleaned would have no application in real life.

"KIDS TODAY!"

I know this sounds like old-fart talk, but I think today's kids are too soft. They have to wear plastic helmets for every outdoor activity but jacking off. Toy safety, car seats, fire-resistant pajamas. Shit! Soft, baby boomer parents, with their cult of the child, are raising a crop of soft, fruity kids.

Here's another example of how adults are training children to be weak. Did you ever notice that every time some guy with an AK-47 shows up in a schoolyard and kills three or four students and a couple of teachers, the next day the school is overrun with psychologists, psychiatrists, grief counselors, and trauma therapists trying to help the children cope? Shit! When I was a kid, if somebody came to our school and killed three or four of us, we went right on with our work. We finished the arithmetic. "Thirty-five classmates, minus four equals thirty-one!" We were tough! I say if a kid can handle the violence in his home, he oughta be able to handle the violence in school.

What bothers me is all this mindless, middlebrow bullshit about children being "our future." So, what's new? Children have always, technically, represented our future. But what does that mean? What is so important about knowing that children are our future? Life as it is right now—today's reality in this country—the people lying on the streets and park benches, living in the dysfunctional homes, the prisons, and the mental institutions, the addicts and drunks and neurotic shoppers, these people were all once children described as "our future." So, this is it, folks. This is what the system produces. The adults you see today are what kids become. Is anything really going to make it any different? To me, they're just another crop of kids waiting to become wage slaves and good little consumers. You know what I see when I look at today's kids? Tomorrow's fucked-up adults.

PARENTAL GUIDANCE

What is all this nonsense about parental guidance, parental control, and parental advisories? The whole reason people in this country are as fucked up as they are and make such ignorant decisions on public policy; is that they listened too closely to their parents in the first place. This is an authoritarian country with too many laws, rules, controls, and restrictions. "Do this! Don't do that! Shut up! Sit still! No talking! Stand up straight!" No wonder kids are so fucked up; traditional authoritarian values. It starts in kindergarten: They give you a coloring book and some crayons, and tell you, "Be creative . . . but don't go outside the lines." Fuck parents!

VOLVO WISDOM

One of the more embarrassing strains of American thought is the liberal-humanist, touchy-feely, warm and fuzzy, New Age, environmental-friendly pseudo-wisdom that appears on bumper stickers: "Have you hugged your kid today?" "Think Globally, Act Locally," and most embarrassing, "Practice Random Kindness and Senseless Acts of Beauty." Isn't that precious? You know, if kindness and beauty require public reminders, maybe it's time we just throw in the jock. Here's another middlebrow abomination: "Our son is an honor student at Franklin School." I'm waiting for a bumper sticker that says, "We have a son in public school who hasn't been shot yet. And he sells drugs to your fuckin' honor student." Or, let's get real: "Our son was a teen suicide because of unrealistic expectations by his father." I think it's time we abandon sentimental, emotional kitsch as a prime means of public expression.

THINGS GO BETTER

I can identify my periods of heavy cocaine use by the years in which I have no idea who was in the World Series or the Superbowl. Bliss.

I remember one Saturday morning when I know I must have been high, because I found myself profoundly moved by Elmer Fudd and Petunia Pig who were appearing in something I took to be a drama.

There was another time when my right nostril was all plugged up, so I spent a whole night snorting in just my left nostril. The weird part is that only my left eye was dilated.

Late one evening, after scraping all the white powder and dust off my dresser top and making two lines out of it, I realized I was actually snorting some Desenex and my own dandruff.

Sometimes I'd get so wired I would do anything to come down a little. You ever chugalug a magnum of children's Tylenol?

Eventually, alas, I realized the main purpose of buying cocaine is to run out of it.

But long after I gave it up I was still self-conscious when I blew my nose in front of other people. And if I had to leave a group of people to go to the bathroom more than once, I was sure everyone thought I was going to do some blow. I used to say, "No, really! I have diarrhea! C'mon! I'll show you."

WE DON'T FEEL GOOD

I've always believed people get the diseases they ask for and deserve. The same is true of countries.

America. Chronic fatigue and anorexia. This is what we've become. "I'm tired!" and, "I don't wanna eat!" How plain. How pathetic. Years ago, a nice, horrifying, fatal consumptive disease would come along and completely eat your fuckin' organs away. Now it's, "I'm tired" and "I don't wanna eat." Christ!

Here's another one: "I'm depressed." Well, shit, look around! Of course you're depressed; you live in a neon sewer. You've earned it. There are supposed to be eleven million clinically depressed Americans. And those are just the ones they know about. I'm sure there are millions more nodding off in closets and attics all across the country. You wanna know why? Because it's one big fuckin' garbage can. At least those people with agoraphobia have found a good solution: "I'm not going out. I don't like it outside."

You say there's rampant cancer? How appropriate. We worship growth; everyone wants growth. Well, we got it. Exuberant cell growth. Lots of big cancers, lots of different kinds and plenty of 'em to go around. All part of who we are. Breast cancer? Who has a more distorted titty hang-up? Epidemic prostate cancer in a nation brimming with assholes? How unusual. Skin cancer? Vanity, thy name is tan. And how 'bout them lungs? The ones that suck up all that fine stuff we belch into the air. We got a cancer for everything. So don't worry, folks, if it's growin' on you, it's a part of the American dream.

Then we have the eating disorders. Is it really a surprise that with all our pathological feeding habits Americans have eating disorders? Who makes worse dietary decisions? Who wastes more food? And not just the ordinary waste of uncaring gluttons; that's easy. I'm talking about those grotesque, all-American food stunts the television news shows find so amusing: hands-behind-the-back pie-eating contests, the largest pizza in the world, the block-long omelet, the biggest banana split ever, the who-can-eat-the-most-hot-peppers-in-fifteen-minutes competition, and the swimming pool full of cherry Jell-O all schlocked up with bad fruit cocktail. And don't forget the wiener-eating contests, where the wieners are actually dipped in water so they'll slide down whole, eliminating all that bothersome chewing. Such healthy attitudes toward food!

And all of this conspicuous, deliberate waste takes place in the midst of global malnutrition and starvation. No wonder fucked-up teenage girls don't want to eat.

Here's another wonderful irony: with all our supposed superiority in food production, we provide our people with far higher rates of stroke, heart attack, colon cancer, and other diet diseases than most "inferior" Third-World food economies do. But don't you worry, those folks are catching up; social pathologies are our biggest export. And so, in a curious way, cancer turns out to be catching, after all.

Please note my restraint in ignoring "shopping disorders."

CONFESSIONS OF A MAGAZINE-OBSESSIVE

I'm always relieved when I see a magazine article I don't have to read, like "How to Turn Prison Rape into a Spiritual Quest." Or "Quesadillas for Quadraplegics." I'm practically giddy when I see an article about a disease I know I'll never get. I laugh heartily as I race past page after page of "Five Hundred Early Warning Signs of Cancer of the Labia." It's such a time-saver.

And I notice as I get older, the magazine articles that catch my eye have begun to change. For instance, in my early twenties, "Ten Career Choices that Lead to Suicide" was a must read. And "Achieving a Six-Hour Orgasm Without a Date" was duly clipped and laminated. But these days I find my interest caught by such titles as "Test Yourself for Alzheimer's," "Ten Tips on Surviving a Nursing Home Fire," and "How to Rid Yourself of Old-Person Smell." I guess the article I really need is "How to Extend Your Magazine Subscriptions Posthumously."

LIMERICKS

There was a young man from St. Maarten

Who saved all his odors from faartin.

If it passed through his crack

It went straight in a sack

And mistakes were all kept in a caarton.

A Jewess who lived in St. Croix

Fell in love with a handsome young goix.

Her parents forbade

She should marry the lad

So instead she eloped with the boix.

A flatulent actor named Barton

Had a lifestyle exceedingly spartan.

Till a playwright one day

Wrote a well-received play

With a part in which Barton could fart in.

KILLER COMIC

It goes without saying I'm not the only person who has noticed this, but I never got to spell it out my way before.

Comedy's nature has two sides. Everybody wants a good time and a couple of laughs, and of course, the comic wants to be known as a real funny guy. But the language of comedy is fairly grim and violent. It's filled with punchlines, gags, and slapstick. After all, what does a comic worry most about? Dying! He doesn't want to die.

"Jeez, I was dyin'. It was like death out there. Like a morgue. I really bombed."

Comics don't want to die, and they don't want to bomb. They want to go over with a bang. And be a real smash. And if everything works out, if they're successful and they make you laugh, they can say, "I killed 'em. I slaughtered those people, I knocked them dead."

And what phrases do we use when we talk about the comic? "He's a riot." "A real scream." "A rib-splitting knee-slapper." "My sides hurt." "My cheeks ache." "He broke me up, cracked me up, slayed me, fractured me, and had me in stitches." "I busted a gut." "I get a real kick out of that guy."

"Laugh? I thought I'd die."